Back to Africa

GEORGE ROSS AND THE MAROONS:
From Nova Scotia to Sierra Leone

Back
to
Africa

George Ross and the Maroons:
From Nova Scotia to Sierra Leone

MAVIS C. CAMPBELL

Africa World Press, Inc.

P.O. Box 1892
Trenton, New Jersey 08607

Africa World Press, Inc.

P.O. Box 1892
Trenton NJ 08607

Cover and Book design by Jonathan Gullery
This book is composed in Caslon

Library of Congress Cataloging-in-Publication Data

Campbell, Mavis Christine
    Back to Africa : George Ross and the Maroons : from Nova Scotia to
Sierra Leone / Mavis C. Campbell.
        p. cm.
    Includes bibliographical references and index.
    ISBN 0-86543-383-6 (HB) : --ISBN 0-86543-384-4 (pbk.)
    1. Maroons--Sierra Leone--History. 2. Ross, George--Diaries. 3. Sierra Leone--
History--To 1896. 4. Back to Africa movement. 5. Jamaicans--Sierra Leone--
History. I. Ross, George. II. Title.
DT516 . 72 . R67A3   1993
966.4--dc20
                                    93-12742
                                        CIP

Dedicated to
Christopher Fyfe
University of Edinburgh

Contents

i
Introduction

xiii
The Ross Journal

xxii
Footnotes

ᔆ
1
THE JOURNAL
ᔆ

79
Appendices

79
Appendix I

87
Appendix II

106
Footnotes

113
Index

INTRODUCTION

F ollowing the tradition that one writer has called a 'Puritan['s] sense of self-scrutiny and introspection that impelled him [Paul Cuffe] to preserve for others a record of his life, thoughts and activities,'[1] George Ross kept a daily diary while en route from Nova Scotia to Sierra Leone with some five hundred and fifty Maroons originally from Trelawny Town in the parish of St. James, Jamaica. These Maroons, all of African descent, fought heroically against the slave system in Jamaica and finally gained their freedom in 1738/9 under formal peace treaties with the government.[2] With quasi-independent Black communities co-existing within the wider slave society relationships, not surprisingly, became increasingly strained until finally in 1795 hostilities broke out between the Trelawny Town Maroons — the largest of these groups — and the colonial state. The result is that they were eventually deported to Nova Scotia after being tricked by the government into laying down arms. Maroon sojourn into Nova Scotia, though fleeting — 1796-1800 — has nevertheless left some lasting impressions.[3]

As might have been expected, the Maroons, coming as they did from the delectable mountainous regions of tropical Jamaica, could not see themselves as destined to reside permanently in Nova Scotia's nordic clime, and they were not reticent in pointing this out to the authorities there. They made their objections known to the colonial authorities, through petitions, memoranda and finally refusal to work until they were sent to a place more like that from which they came. The moment was timely for them, for a back to Africa movement was afoot in Britain, and they were soon sent to Sierra Leone. And it was George Ross, an employee of the Sierra Leone Company, who was commissioned while on sick leave in London to supervise the transportation of these Maroons from Nova Scotia to Freetown in Sierra Leone, where they arrived in September 1800.

The British practice of sending black people back to Africa should be seen in context. In the initial stage this was based on the same reasoning as that of the Americans in attempting to repatriate their blacks to Africa. The primary concern of the Americans was a horror of having an independent United States of America with blacks as free citizens on a basis of equality with the whites. Thomas Jefferson, for one, supported repatriation as preferable to the conversion of blacks into serfs — a choice which showed clearly that he did not even conceive the notion of equality as a probability. Jefferson had a great aversion to America's becoming a mongrel nation which to him was a 'degradation to which no lover of his country, no lover of excellence in the human character can innocently consent.'[4] He was indifferent as to where they were to be sent, so long as they were at a distance from the whites, beyond the bounds of miscegenation. To Haiti, perhaps: and since this country's example had already precipitated a slave uprising in his native Virginia, then Toussaint Louverture might well be willing to take off America's hands a few of her rebellious blacks. But nothing came of this plan. To Brazil, perhaps: but then, Jefferson's overture to Portugal on this measure also proved abortive.[5] Other suggestions to expatriate the American blacks to Haiti and other places were also made by different people at different times,[6] but 'back to Africa' was the most insistent cry.

The original back to Africa plan in Britain was predicated upon considerations of race and economy. Britain had a few blacks in her midst, mostly from Africa, from around the middle of the sixteenth century. But as the Atlantic slave trade expanded steadily during the seventeenth and eighteenth centuries the black presence in Britain increased enormously, and by the third quarter of the latter century they were computed (probably by conjecture) to have been between ten and twenty thousand.[7] These blacks consisted of those who served in the British Navy and were eventually discharged, invariably without compensation; those (mostly mulatto slaves) who accompanied their absentee masters from the British West Indies, and those who were brought into the country by captains of slave ships. But probably the greatest single influx of blacks into Britain came as a result of the termination of the American War of Independence in 1783. Under the recent soubriquet, 'black loyalists,' they constituted some of those Afro-Americans who fought with Britain and were finally discharged from the British army and navy after the war.

The increased black population in Britain became a source of alarm for those preoccupied with racial 'purity,' as it was a source of genuine concern for those interested in human distress. Even before the influx of the American blacks, there were loud cries in Britain against the black presence — all based on identical reasoning to that of Jefferson's.

Especially after Lord Mansfield's decision in the Somerset case (1772), which said, in paraphrase, that a master could not reclaim a former slave while in England, many in Britain, fearing that additional blacks would arrive to proclaim themselves 'free,' implored the deportation of those already in the country: by such an act, 'the race of Britons [would be preserved] from stain and contamination.][8] Some nervously saw in every town and in 'almost every village...a little race of mulattoes, mischievous as monkeys, and infinitely more dangerous.'[9] Edward Long, who was later to write his famous History of Jamaica (3 volumes), angered at the Mansfield decision, said, in part, in his tract on the case, that 'in the course of a few generations more, the English blood will become so contaminated with this mixture [that] the whole nation [will] resemble the Portuguese and Moriscos in complexion of skin and baseness of mind. This is a venomous and dangerous ulcer that threatens to disperse its malignancy far and wide, until every family catches infection from it.[10] The London Chronicle of March 13-16,1773 (one year after the Somerset case), echoing Long, hoped that 'Parliament will provide such remedies as may be adequate to the occasion, by expelling Blacks now here,. . . and prohibiting the introduction of them in this kingdom for the future, and save the natural beauty of Britons from the Morisco tint.'

Others were more alarmed by what they perceived as the indigence of these people. They saw them as constituting a potentially heavy burden on the welfare of the country. Unable to obtain employment after service in the army and the navy, and with their inflated number after 1783, most of them were soon reduced to the greatest distress.

Their distress was due almost wholly to the invidious distinctions made between them and the white loyalists who arrived in England, where invariably whites were given assistance by the British government while the blacks were mostly refused when they made their claims. The British officials dealing with the situation, were quite candid about their discriminatory practices, arguing that the Afro-Americans should regard themselves as fortunate to have been in a country like Britain where they would not be reconsigned to a state of slavery. This was precisely what they told a Connecticut black — as well as myriad others — who petitioned for claims. [11]

As the years passed, their misery became alarming. This was especially so in the streets of London where they could be found as reflected in the news media of the period, emaciated and forlorn, and in a state of beggary. In addition to the blacks, there were also starving Indians, abandoned by returning Nabobs from India, all wretched in a strange land, 'cold,hungry, naked, friendless.'[12] From this period, the British government's overriding aim was to evacuate them from England by any means whatever.

The opportunity offered itself when Henry Smeathman, a well-travelled adventurer, presented a plan to the Committee for the Relief of the 'Black Poor' — established by some private individuals in England to relieve this group — to settle these people in Sierra Leone. It would appear to have been of no consequence to the Committee and to the government officials that Smeathman had, a year earlier, argued against sending convicts to Sierra Leone on the grounds that they would soon die like flies, for the British government accepted the plan when it was presented to them. In due course (April 1787), after much coercion and false promises to the blacks by the officials, 411 or 441 'Black Poor' sailed for Sierra Leone.[13]

In all this, Granville Sharp stood out like a beacon in what was a most callous deportation as the final solution for the black problem. Since 1783 when their numbers increased dramatically in England, Sharp began to envisage a settlement plan for Africans back to the land of their forefathers. Upon being consulted therefore, by the London blacks about the scheme — 'sometimes they came in large bodies together' [14] — and when the unscrupulous Smeathman solicited his support, he jumped at the idea. Perceiving the scheme in the wider context of the 'Province of Freedom,' Sharp organized it on these lines as a personal venture of his own: 'By the end of 1788 he reckoned he had spent altogether £1,735.18.8 on the Province of Freedom.'[15] Thus while the Committee for the Relief of the Black Poor and the British government saw the blacks in their misery as an embarrassing nuisance to be rid of by any means. Sharp saw the venture as an experiment in 'freedom' for the blacks of the diaspora who were the casualty of European enslavement ever since the Portuguese first penetrated the West Coast of Africa in the fifteenth century.

In the process, Granville Sharp's idea prevailed for a time, and other like-minded men gave him much support. These included, among others, Thomas Clarkson who had dedicated his life to the abolition of the slave trade, and William Wilberforce, certainly not nearly of the same humanitarian 'class' (although history has probably given him a disproportionate share of encominums on this score). Some of these supporters were to become members of the Committee for the

Abolition of the Slave Trade, formed in 1787.

Named the 'Province of Freedom' originally, now Freetown in addition to adjoining districts, the newly-found territory, very self-consciously announced its intent. But the settlement, conceived by Sharp as a kind of eighteenth century enlightened utopia, soon failed and by 1790 it hardly existed.'[16] Undaunted, Sharp and others like himself as well as others more interested in business and commerce in Africa, soon helped to found the Sierra Leone Company (1791). This Company, which governed Sierra Leone until 1800 when this country was instituted into a Crown Colony, had a Board of Directors under a chairman in London and a Governor and Council and other officials in Sierra Leone. George Ross was one of these officials. He began as a clerk, December 10, 1795, (see Appendix 1, Letter 1), was soon promoted to Cashier of the Company, and was appointed Alderman (which rather amused him; see his entry of 12th October, 1800) within the terms of the Charter that instituted Sierra Leone into a colony, under the jurisdiction of the Sierra Leone Company.

Some of the officials of the Sierra Leone Company also paid lip-service to the philanthropic ideas of Sharp and others like Thomas Clarkson and Wilberforce who were among the Directors of the Company. Participation in the slave trade for instance was to be strictly forbidden. However, many employees of the Company did become active slavers while so employed, while many left their employment to become engaged in the lucrative trade on the West African Coast.

In looking around for more settlers — since many of the 'Black Poor' had died or deserted — the Company was happy to admit another group before the Maroons came on the scene. These were the Afro-Americans who won their freedom by fighting, as did some of the Black Poor, on the British side during the American War of Independence. They were first sent to Nova Scotia but when the promises of land and other perquisites that were made to them by the British were not kept, they made representations in England. This was a most propitious time when the sentiments of the enlightenment led by Sharp and the abolitionists, or the 'Clapham set,' or 'sect' or 'the Saints' in England were bent on reclaiming not only the blacks of the diaspora, but also the continent of Africa. By 1792 some 1,190 of them sailed for Sierra Leone, supervised in this case by John Clarkson (brother of Thomas Clarkson) who also kept a daily journal. Thus the Maroons under Ross' supervision took the same course that these Afro-Americans ('Nova Scotions, in Sierra Leone history) — or 'fugitives from...the Revolutionary War' (according to Jefferson),[17] had taken eight years before.

Jefferson notwithstanding, it should be noted that a number of these fugitives from the American Revolutionary War, was born in Africa, some remembering having been kidnapped in the manner of Alex Haley's Kunta Kinte. One such found himself after fifteen years 'nearly on the spot from whence he had been carried off,...pointing to a particular part of the beach, where, as he relates, a woman laid hold of him, he being then a boy, and sold him to an American slave-ship in the river.'[18] And as if to give credence to his story, a few days later some 'Natives' came to look at the new settlers out of curiosity, and among them was 'an elderly woman' who recognized her son who had been kidnapped some fifteen years ago. After an emotional reunion, the Afro-American rejoined his family among the Mende people of Sierra Leone.[19]

The fourth group of blacks — and the largest in number — who were sent to Sierra Leone were the 'liberated Africans' or 'recaptives.' These were Africans bound for the New World as slaves, who, after the 'illegalisation' of the slave trade in 1808, were rescued as 'contraband' from illicit slave traders by the British. Although the majority of these recaptives went to Sierra Leone, a few found their way to Cuba and some of the British islands of the region.[20]

These four groups, the Black Poor from Britain, the Afro-Americans, the Maroons and the Recaptives or Liberated Africans, were expected to transmit Western civilization to Africa. But the Company Directors initially, and later the British government, did not leave the process to chance. This is in contrast to the suggestion of Jefferson — unrealistic at best, cynical at worst —when in 1802 he made his minister in London approach the Sierra Leone Company to negotiate — unsuccessfully — the transportation of American blacks to the newly found British Colony. Jefferson felt that these returning ex-slaves of America would 'carry back to the country of their origin, the seeds of civilization which might render their sojournment and suffering here a blessing in the end to that country [sic].'[21]

Realizing the need for much 'social engineering,' to suit their· scheme of things, the British, for their part, proceeded to encourage these black groups, through their administration, the missionary societies, the educational system, and the ethic of rewards and penalties, to become totally immersed in Western value-systems and status patterns. The British philanthropists were joyous about the scheme. Wilberforce, for instance, wrote to Talleyrand to say that 'Sierra Leone was settled with a view to promote the arts, and the blessings of civilized life, amongst the natives of Africa.'[22] The directors of the Sierra Leone Company saw the motive which led them so readily to the settling of the Maroons as the same as that which had induced them to accept the 1,190 Nova Scotians: 'to civilize Africa and to lessen the evils of the slave trade.' They were anxious to raise the Maroon —particularly the children — 'in the scale of human beings by taking them under our wings and whatever expense we may advise or authority we may desire will be merely with a view to this end.'[23]

But, as usual, British humanitarianism had an uncanny knack of stalking in propinquity with mammon. And the very next sentence of the directors revealed this trait. The directors hoped that the Governor and Council of Sierra Leone would 'not be unmindful of Oeconomy [sic] nor disposed improperly to indulge the indolence to be expected in these Settlers.'[24]

In fact, a colony with a group of grateful blacks, carefully nurtured along Western lines, holding themselves aloof from the autochthons, and living in symbiotic relationship with them is a model of colonial *divide et imperium*. The British in a controlling position would find this colony of immense economic and strategic importance especially when it is noted that the founding of this territory coincided with new thinking on Africa. Those who projected the new industrial needs of Europe soon saw Africa's economic potentialities as greater than that which the slave trade had already yielded. Sierra Leone itself, as a British colony, was to prove somewhat disappointing as an economic proposition — as it was for the Sierra Leone Company earlier. But its real importance was strategic. Possessing a magnificent harbour, the best in West Africa, it was to become a British naval base after 1808.

'Legitimate' trade with Africa was to become the order of the day and the African Institution which superseded the Sierra Leone Company had this as its primary consideration. To be sure, it articulated other goals, all reflecting the highmindedness of the age. The directors, with the Duke of Gloucester, nephew of George III, as the Institutions' first president, claimed to have been 'anxious' to 'adopt such measures as are best calculated to promote... [the native African's] civilization and happiness'[25] -and a host of other such high-sounding shibboleths. But in essence, the goal was trade with Africa. Africa was to be geared to the husbandry of agriculture, producing

critical commodities which Britain could not, to satisfy her burgeon-
ing industries. Palm oil, for instance, was invaluable as it served a
quadrupled purpose within the context of Britain's Industrial
Revolution. The oil was useful to lubricate the new industrial
machines. It was made into soap to cleanse Britain's working population made greasy by the teeming factories. It was used for culinary
purposes, and it was also used in candle-making to give light to the
factories, religious and other public places, as well as domestic estab-
lishments. In return, England was to create demands on the entire
African continent, if possible, for her manufactured goods.

Ever since the loss of 'the 13 colonies,' Britain knew she was in
need of expanded markets. A classical mercantilist web with Africa
was being woven — fashioned at this period to suit the necessities of
the new industrial order which superseded the commercial epoch
that for Britain had been based on the slave trade.

Ironically, one of the first and most eloquent exponents of the new
economic thinking — or legitimate trade with Africa — was Olaudah
Equiano, or Gustavus Vassa (his European name). Equiano, an Ibo
from Nigeria, was kidnapped as a child and taken to the West Indies
into slavery but ultimately he made his way to England as a free man.
Here he became a foremost abolitionist, working closely with
Granville Sharp and William Wilberforce, among others. In this capacity, Equiano was appointed Commissary to supervise the transportation of the Black Poor to Sierra Leone, which, we already noted, was
sponsored largely by Sharp. Equiano, however, was soon summarily
dismissed for exposing fraudulent practices against these poor people even before the vessel left England. Equiano's autobiography, *The
Interesting Narrative of the Life of Olaudah Equiano, or Gustavus Vassa,
the African, written by Himself* (London: 10 Union Street, 1789), is a
standard source material for a glimpse of slavery in West Africa, but
more especially, for a poignant account of the Middle Passage of the
European slave trade.

In the same year Equiano published his autobiography, the Lords
of the Committee of the Privy Council in Britain, acting as the Board
of Trade, was conducting serious investigations into 'the present state
of the Trade in Africa, and particularly the Trade in Slaves.' Equiano
had strong views on the issue and soon sent in his report which was
to become 'one of the strongest economic arguments against the slave
trade (and) was also used by the promoters of the Sierra Leone
Company.'[26] His report ran (with its inconsistent orthography):

My Lord (Hawkesbury),
As the illicit Traffic of Slavery is to be taken into the Consideration of the British Legislature, I have taken the Liberty of sending you the following Sentiments, which have met the Approbation of many intelligent and commercial Gentlemen.

Sir,
A System of Commerce once being established in Africa, the Demand for Manufactories will most rapidly augment, as the native Inhabitants will insensibly adopt our Fashions, Manners, Customs, etc. etc.

In proportion to the Civilization, so will be the Consumption of British Manufactures...
The Abolition of diabolical Slavery will give a most rapid and permanent Extension to Manufacturers, which is totally and diametrically opposite to what some interested People assert.
The Manufactories of this Country must and will in the Nature and Reason of Things have a full and constant Employ by supplying the African Markets. The Population, Bowels, and Surface of Africa abound in valuable and useful Returns; the hidden Treasuries of Countries will be brought to Light and into Circulation.
Industry, Enterprise and Mining will have their full Scope, proportionately as they civilize. In a word it lays open an endless Field of Commerce to the British manufacturer and Merchant Adventurer...
Europe contains One hundred and Twenty Millions of Inhabitants; Query, How many Millions doth Africa contain? Supposing the Africans, collectively and individually, to expend Five Pounds a Head in Raiment and Furniture yearly, when civilized etc. — an Immensity beyond the Reach of Imagination: This I conceive to be a Theory founded upon Facts; and therefore an infallible One. If the Blacks were permitted to remain in their own Country they would double themselves every Fifteen Years: In Proportion to such Increase would be the Demand for Manufactures. Cotton and Indigo grow spontaneously in some Parts of Africa: A Consideration this of no small Consequence to the manufacturing Towns of Great Britain.
The Chamber of Manufactories of Great Britain, held in London, will be strenuous in the Cause. It opens a most immense, glorious, and happy Prospect.

The Cloathing, etc. of a Continent Ten thousand Miles in Circumference, and immensely rich in productions of every Denomination, would make an interesting Return indeed for our Manufactories, a free Trade being established...[27]

Equiano's mercantilist thesis combined with the civilizing mission of trade was to be re-echoed by many writers and politicians after him. Thomas Fowell Buxton, for instance, writing in 1839, proclaimed that 'Africa is, indeed, encircled by an effectual barrier against the entrance of commerce, cultivation, and Christianity. That barrier is the Slave Trade,'[28] which, by this time, was carried out by Cuba, Brazil and the United States of America in the New World.

The Maroons and the other immigrant blacks of Freetown as well as the 'Natives' were thus vigorously encouraged to pursue agriculture. And the fervor with which the colonial department, led especially by the Duke of Portland and some of the Governors of this colony, preached the importance of agriculture soon made this occupation appear a prerequisite for the civilization the blacks were promised.

Portland's letters to the Governor of Nova Scotia, upon the occasion of the Maroons' expatriation to Sierra Leone, imperiously ordered the Governor to see to it that the Maroons take with them their 'implements of agriculture' or implements of husbandry.'[29]

One of Governor Thompson's letters from Sierra Leone to Whitehall on the subject stands out among many of its kind. Supporting the abolition of the slave trade on purely economic grounds, the Governor argued that every 'native of Africa who should be taken out of this colony would give a sensible blow to the interests of Great Britain in this part of Africa. The Natives of Africa, my Lord, are our Sinews; and it will be in vain that the lifeblood of the British Enterprize and speculation is put in circulation if we are crippled in this particular.'[30] With the new thinking, and in line with mercantilism, manufacture of all kinds was discouraged: 'The employing or allowing to be employed any Male Native of Africa in any Crafts or Employment other than the Cultivation of the Ground, in the present circumstances of this Colony, would be utterly ruinous, and the source of every kind of Mischief...God forbid that the introduction of Natives of Africa to trades and Crafts should ever be permitted to increase;...the cultivation of land is the grand object.'[31]

It is interesting to note that Paul Cuffe's 'back to Africa' plans approximated closely to the new thinking about this continent. Paul Cuffe (1759-1817), 'an extraordinary phenomenon — a black man who was a wealthy man of property, a petitioner for equal rights for blacks, owner of a fleet of vessels, an able sea captain, founder of a public school, a devout Quaker, friend of President James Madison,' [32] sponsored some 38 Afro-Americans' return to Africa (Freetown) eleven years after Ross landed at the same port with the Maroons.

Cuffe, the Afro-American, strongly believed that Africa was in need of moral rehabilitation and, to him, the best means by which this could be done was through Western values — Christianity and industry. And Cuffe, possessing these 'acceptable' virtues in abundance was convinced, initially, that is, before his visits to Sierra Leone, that he would be instrumental in bringing light to Africa. 'If I could wish to be made use of,' he wrote to a friend on his second voyage to Sierra Leone in April 1816, 'to improve the morals of the inhabitants of Africa, I am sorry to say that subject when I at first entered upon appears must fail.'[33] Cuffe's disappointment, expressed in his singular style, it can be surmised, reflected the disappointing state of trade he encountered in Freetown, and the general social and moral malaise of the colony.[34] But Cuffe was prolific in dispensing Bibles to Sierra Leonans. To King Tom of the Temme, who appeared to Cuffe 'sober and grave,' he gave a Bible, a history of slavery written by Elizabeth Webb, a Quaker, and other books. He also gave to the king a pamphlet accompanied 'with a letter of advice from myself such as appeared to me to be good to hand to the king for the use and encouragement of the nations of Africa.'[35] Another source was more explicit about the nature of this advice. In addition to the gifts mentioned, Cuffe also gave the king an essay on avoiding war. And then he gave what he considered appropriate advice for a head of state such as King Tom, for the use and encouragement of Africans. He expressed ethical principles with a view to inculcating a civilized way of life for Africans who should be sober, 'by doing justly, loving mercy, and walking humbly.' Youth should be shielded from 'corruptions of the world' like swearing, bad company, and spirituous liquor, and so forth. To King George of the Bullom, Cuffe gave also a Bible, a testament, and other religious writings.[36]

It is certain that Cuffe's [37] Afro-Americans soon intermingled with their compatriots, the Nova Scotians and most probably with the Maroons also. After the first few years of acute tensions between them — arising from the fact that the Maroons, at the time of their arrival in Freetown, were largely responsible for the successful suppression of the Nova Scotians' rebellion against the Company—the lives of these two groups soon became intimately interrelated. The realities of the larger society of Sierra Leone soon transcended group solidarity. This is a little known aspect of some of the linkages among African, Afro-American and Caribbean history.

Accepting the challenge of the highly competitive and closely-knit Freetown polity, the Maroons and the Nova Scotians, through business association and marriage, soon became the very cornerstone of the Creoles of Sierra Leone. They distinguished themselves in trade, business, the professions and leadership positions and not in agriculture as the British had planned. They were, however, soon outnumbered by the recaptives who were also to become part of the Creole society. The outstanding achievements of the Maroons of Sierra Leone, with their numerous 'firsts' will be dealt with in a separate work.

THE ROSS JOURNAL

Ross began his Journal in mid-Atlantic from September 1800 and he kept up the practice when he landed in Sierra Leone and was appointed Superintendent of the Maroons. This badly punctuated document, with its original spelling, its syntactic peculiarities, its ungrammatical construction in part and its disconcerting abbreviations is nevertheless a most important source on the history of the Maroon people and on the early history of Sierra Leone.

Ross' Journal gives almost what could be considered an ethnographic account of the Maroons which the official documents could not do — and did not intend to do. Apart from the fact that Ross had a Chaucer-like interest in human behavior, it was a part of his official instruction from the Directors of the Sierra Leone Company 'to acquire also knowledge of their [the Maroons'] capacities, dispositions, manners and customs...'[37] To accomplish this as well as to explain the terms on which the Maroons were to be received in Sierra Leone, Ross embarked to Nova Scotia and lived with them at Maroon Hall, a most important center of Maroon activities, for nearly a year. He was thus in the capacity of the observer-participant, and there is no doubt that by the time he reached Sierra Leone, Ross had a pretty thorough knowledge of Maroon life-style.

Ross introduces us to, inter alia, the funeral practices of the Maroons, who were, for the most part, originally of the Akan speaking group of Ghana. We are also made aware of their ceremonial practices upon the birth of a child. Much rum was consumed on both occasions, and the Maroons expected some rum to be given to them at such times, as of right, as a part of their allowance. All this depicted to Ross, the European, a mode of behavior which seemed strange indeed. We note his bafflement in his entry of Friday, October 24, 1800: 'Mary — Bob Brown's daughter died today. Gave 1/2 gallon of Rum for her burial — Strange that Maroons should be sure to get drunk on the death of their nearest relatives. Witness Bob Brown, Sam Shaw and Ellis.'

R.S. Rattery, in his careful works on the Ashanti people, established that rum was indeed served on funeral occasions, but this was followed only after all concerned had fasted throughout the day 'and as a considerable quantity of liquor was consumed the effect of this showed on a number of people. Much of the intoxication noticed by Europeans on such occasions...is due to the fact that those participating have been fasting for long periods, so that even a little liquor soon goes to the head. Moreover, indulgence on such occasions only takes place after the solemn rites have been performed and after all the serious business of the day is over.'[38]

Ross seemed to have come to terms with the fact that the practice of consuming rum was not only to commemorate a birth but also to 'celebrate' a death. His subsequent impassive entries such as, 'Harding's daughter, being but of yesterday, was put off with half a Gallon'; or that which gave Captain Gray 1/2 Gallon for his Grandson, 'dropt this morning,' may well bewilder the casual reader for its incomprehensibility.

The Journal has given some excellent insights into the traditional Maroon attitude to land—a resource factor which, in the perception of the Maroons, was never intended to be alienated from the collectivity of a people. And, as a corollary, they found the idea of paying taxes or rent on land unthinkable. They were asked to do so in Freetown. The confrontation between certain Maroon leaders and the British Governor and his party over this matter in Sierra Leone is a classical example of cultural non-communication. It should be noted that the Afro-Americans who preceded the Maroons to Freetown had also strenuously resisted the paying of quit rent, and ironically, it was the imposition of quit rents by the authorities in Sierra Leone on the Afro-Americans (Nova Scotians) that had provoked them into the rebellion that the Maroons had helped to suppress. This resulted in much initial tension, fear and hostility between these two groups as hinted above, but the irony is that the attitude of both groups to land policy sprang from the same source-their African heritage.

In Ross's *Journal*, Maroon personalities came to life. It is thus a primary repository for some of the biographies of outstanding personalities from the Maroons who left Jamaica for Nova Scotia and finally for Sierra Leone. Quite a few Creoles of Sierra Leone today can trace their roots through this *Journal*.

Let us take a closer look at old Colonel Montague James (promoted to the rank of Colonel in Nova Scotia), the last chief of the Trelawny Town Maroons who were first ruled by Cudjoe of the Treaty. Dallas for one, sees Captain Montague James as hardly more than a pathetic figure of fun, wearing 'a gaudy, laced, red coat, and a gold-laced hat with a plume of feathers. None but their captains and officers sat in his presence, except upon the ground. He was the first helped at meals; no woman ate with him, and he was waited on by the young men. He presided in the councils, and exercised an authoritative tone of voice to enforce order, which, however, he seldom effected; for he was, in fact, considered in no better light than as an old woman, but to whom the shadow of respect was to be paid, as he bore the title of Chief.'[39] Curiously, documents consulted in Jamaica, Canada, England and Sierra Leone, including Ross' journal itself, all seem to contradict this old woman profile of James. We know that Montague became Captain of the Trelawny Town Maroons, possibly around the latter part of the 1770s at a time when John James was the white superintendent of this town. From the evidence, both men got along very well indeed. When John James, for his outstanding service to the government, in keeping the Maroons of Trelawny Town in such good order and 'proper subjection,' was appointed major-commandant of all the Maroon communities in the island, 1779, Montague James assumed a special role in this town. Although his title was still that of Captain, he was granted a special commission around 1781 to act under James in Trelawny Town to ease Major James of his enormously increased duties. From this time, Montague James is referred to in the documents, as 'assistant superintendent of Trelawyn Town.' Apparently Montague held this position until 1792 except for about eighteen months, when he was absent from the island for the recovery of his health. We do not know where he went but it is stated in a petition that his health was greatly impaired for being frequently out in parties with the Maroons in search of runaway slaves. As far as we know no other Maroon leader had assumed this position for which he was paid a special salary by the government. Maroon leaders were not paid by the government; only the white residents were so paid, by the terms of the Treaties. In 1782 for instance, the house of Assembly voted Montague 100 pounds as assistant superintendent of Trelawny Town. But apparently Montague had some difficulty in collecting an annual salary — not an unusual problem for office holders, including white resident Maroon superintendents of the period. We also find John James sending a number of petitions to the Assembly on his and on Montague's behalf. Between 1782 and 1788 for example, according to one of James' petitions, Montague received only the sum of 100 pounds mentioned above, yet both men have served to the 'utmost.' This petition yielded Montague another 200 pounds, a sum which was comparable to the salary of the regular superintendents of the other Maroon towns. In this instance Montague had problems collecting this amount from the receiver general, although, James' petition of November 1790 emphasized that Montague had continued to exert himself with every 'diligent attention.' The Assembly again felt that he 'ought to be paid' and voted him the sum of 200 pounds, for his services for 1790. How Montague fared in the years not mentioned since 1782 is not clear but by 1792 there was decidedly a less friendly attitude to him and to the other Maroons in general. In reply to another of Major James's petitions on his and Montague's behalf, in December 1792, the Assembly recommended to disagree with Montague's claim for an annual salary, arguing that the warrant or commission granted to him in 1781 was 'highly improper' and 'illegal,' and instead of encouraging him by rewards, the house should rather discontinue the practice. All this foreshadowed the attitude that led to the Trelawny Town/ government war there years later (1795) and their eventual deportation.[40] Montague James was a principal actor in these events and he led his people first to Nova Scotia and then to Sierra Leone. From Nova Scotia he sent numerous petitions to the government protesting against residing in a cold country like Nova Scotia until finally they were sent to Sierra Leone under Ross' supervision. And it is from Ross' journal that we first see him at close quarters. A judicious, even-tempered and wise old man, referred to mostly as 'the General' throughout the *Journal*. Ross relied on him heavily when making decisions relative to Maroon affairs. We even find Montague in an apparent state of mild inebriety chanting old "Coromantyn' songs, which suggests that Montague may have been of the Akan speaking group. But unfortunately, since it became the general practice for Maroon leaders particularly to adopt the names of prominent planters after the Treaties, it is impossible to identify their ethnic origins given the change of names.

Montague was so esteemed in Sierra Leone that he was probably the first citizen of this country to have received from the government what could be called an old age pension. On March 26, 1801, the Governor and Council moved that 'in consideration of the meritorious conduct, increasing bodily infirmities, and destitute condition of Colonel Montague James of the Maroons, (be it) resolved that in addition to the ration of provisions which he now received in common with the rest of the Maroons, a pension of One Dollar per week be paid him by the Accountant to commence from the 21st day of April 1801; and that the Superintendent be requested to communicate this resolution to Colonel Montague.'[41] On the 2nd of June of the same year, the Governor and Council again moved that 'by the good conduct' of Colonel Montague, they were desirous to relieve the infirmities of his old age, and ordered that 'the Superintendent of the Maroons be requested to take him into his house to board, on an allowance of 50 pounds sterling per annum.'[42] Ten days later this same body moved that the Superintendent of the Maroons be authorized to supply the Colonel with a 'few necessary articles of household furniture.'

Old Montague is also made immortal by A.B.C. Sibthorpe, who, in his *History of Sierra Leone*, (1868) mentioned Montague under his *Names of Note* in Sierra Leone (p.15).

Then there is old Major Jarrett. As Montague was equable in temperament so was Major Jarrett irascible, temperamental, quarrelsome and was constantly at loggerheads with Ross and the Maroon leaders. Yet, a more engaging character, it is difficult to find, as seen from his numerous feuds with Ross. And Ross could not help observing, after being repeatedly exasperated with Jarrett, that he was 'a fine fellow...when he chooses to conduct himself well; he is a great Man in great matters; he acts nobly and if he is engaged in small matters, his genius and manners is such that by foul means or fair, he makes them of consequence.'[43]

Nash Hamilton quarreled with Ross about his lot of land, accusing the Superintendent of partiality to Captain Smith. The proprietor of the 'Maroon Bar' in Freetown, opened 1972? was proud of his Maroon ancestry (in conversation with him during field work), and Nash Hamilton may well be his ancestor.

The Thorpes, a distinguished Freetown family with many 'firsts' is well featured in Ross' *Journal*. The first 'document' in a Maroon handwriting discovered by this author is by John Thorpe. Here young Thorpe was a school boy in Nova Scotia, transcribing in his best script,

God gives us the greatest Encouragement to be good, by promising us more Happiness than we
can express, or all the World can afford; and
he also declares, that if we continue in Sin,
and disobey him, he will punish us forever and
ever. If then, neither these Promises nor

Threatenings will do, we are unavoidably lost.—
Pitch upon such a Course of Life as is excellent
and praiseworthy.——

John Thorpe, Maroon School
Preston, August 15, 1799[44]

The precepts involved, were meant, no doubt, to equip the young man with a new point of view since the *old* Maroons had stoutly refused to be handicapped by Christianity or by British education while in Nova Scotia, but they did not object to the *young* being so socialized. This young Thorpe may have been the uncle of another John Thorpe Fyfe mentioned, as the 'first from the colony to enter a university institution' (University College, London) in 1832 to study Natural Philosophy and Law.[45] It is not clear whether he is the same 'John Thorpe, the first Sierra Leonean, a Maroon,...(to be) called to the English Bar in 1850,'[46] in Porter's work.

'Poor Palmer's Dog!' Ross wrote, 'And poor Palmer — after giving his poor dog a part of his own allowance all the way from Nova Scotia, to be the first night after landing devoured by a ravenous leopard!' and this Palmer may well be the old forebear of the enterprising and successful businessman, Nicholas Palmer with his chain of Drug Stores in Freetown in the 1970s. Then there are the Shaws and the Hardings who intermarried and a descendant, Charles Shaw Harding, was to donate the land for the Maroon Church in Freetown and which was made an historical landmark in the 1970s.

These are only a few of the characters to be met with in Ross' Journal whose descendants are still living in Sierra Leone today.

In some respects, Ross' Journal may also claim to belong to the genre of slave traders' Journals in the sense that Ross dabbled in the trade on his return journey home to Britain. And he has left us some interesting price listings of slaves on the West Coast of Africa, and lists of trade goods connected with the slave trade. In the Journal we also encounter one of the few instances of a successful slave mutiny during the Atlantic slave trade. A creature of his age, Ross shows no moral attitude whatsoever to slavery.

Ross himself comes out of the Journal as rather an extraordinary person — witty, in a matter-of-fact way, seemingly well-balanced and rather prosaic; but honest and frank — qualities which the Maroons have always appreciated. His interaction with them, though rocky at times, was, on the whole, successful, — which could not be said of most other Europeans interacting with them, with the outstanding exception of Major James in Jamaica. Ross' success may well be partly due to his preparatory stay with them in Nova Scotia.

Ross was not without the ethnocentricism so characteristic of European attitudes of Africa and Africans of the period. Yet his account of the Maroons — a people with a culture so different from his own — showed relatively little condescension. This is remarkable especially because of his low status in white ranking order, where this category in a position of authority in the 'colonies', can often be rather supercilious. But Ross' previous behavior, with Peter Francis is more in character. Francis, a Nova Scotian (Afro-American) was put in charge of raising a militia in Sierra Leone and the Europeans involved, among whom was Ross, took exception, Ross himself thinking it degrading.[47] Ross' attitude to the Maroons, on the other hand, even when he was always determined to show that he was in charge, displayed the same mixture of genuine respect, awe and exasperated affection shown by most of the British administrators who dealt with them in Nova Scotia and in Sierra Leone. In Nova Scotia they were exposed not only to the exaggerated protectiveness — bordering on possessiveness — of Sir John Wentworth, then lieutenant governor of that territory, but they also had Prince Edward, the Duke of Kent, commander-in-Chief of Nova Scotia, praising the 'smartly dressed body of men.' Likewise, in Sierra Leone, some of the governors, indiscreetly, perhaps, showed them off favourably against the Nova Scotians. All this was most certainly due to the awe the Maroons inspired because of their great reputation as warriors — not unlike the same kind of respect the British had for the Gurkhas of India.

It is not clear whether Ross was required to keep a daily journal by the Sierra Leone Company as was the practice with most trading companies of the period. The East India Company, for instance, required the master of a ship and the first and second mates to keep journals which must be handed over to the company after each voyage. Such journals were primarily records of winds, currents and temperatures, accounts of all lands and ships sighted, records of the general condition of the crew, signs of disaffection or mutinies and the like. Even if the Sierra Leone Company did not require a journal from Ross, he, nevertheless, paid much attention to the above subjects.

Ross also fits the typology of Europeans of the period who travelled to Africa. Generally self-centered and individualistic, many Scottish, who sought Africa for a combination of reasons: to better their condition, to visit far-off exotic places and to seek adventure. A number of these had education that did not go beyond the parish or the burgh school of Scotland, and the grammar school of England. Ross, who was obviously from Edinburgh (see his entry of 19th November), was probably a product of the Scottish burgh. The quality of the journal would certainly not earn him a place in the literary hall of fame. It is just barely literate, clumsy for the most part, and with no claim to elegance of style. Yet Ross was obviously fairly well read. This is borne out by his many direct and in some cases, indirect allusions to some literary classics. Parts of the journal also showed a trained regard for the meticulous recording of trade goods with prices, weights or amounts neatly listed. It may well have been this propensity that landed him the position of cashier of the Sierra Leone Company in 1797. Ross refused at first, on grounds of health and because of the great risks connected with the post. His salary was then only One Hundred Pounds per year — and anyone living in the Colony, he reasoned, would know that it was not 'more than sufficient to furnish him decently with the bare demands of life.' But Ross was firmly prevailed upon by Governor and Council to accept the post. 'Did they not consider him as possessing a more than common accuracy, they should not have nominated him to such an Office.'[48]

In editing the Journal, I have tried to retain some of Ross' original spellings when they can be easily understood by the general reader; for example, 'staid' for stayed, 'chuse' for choose and the like; but I have altered others which may have proved daunting. I have also inserted most of the required punctuations which were of no concern to Ross at all. The excessive use of capitals has also been amended, and most of the numerous abbreviations have been expanded: 'fm' for fathom, 'sd' for said, 'hand-f' for handerchief, 'ye' for the, among many others. The dating of entries has been standardized.

I have scrupulously tried not to alter the content and the sense of the journal and in dealing with the textual difficulties I tried as much as possible not to allow my editorial intrusions to affect its original flavor. In a few cases I have retained some rather convoluted sentence structures to give the full flavor of Ross' writing (see a part of his entry of 2nd November). A paraphrase is given in square brackets. As much as possible too, I have tried to avoid the excessive use of the devise ('sic'), as this would tend to clutter the text unnecessarily.

Editorial comments (in square brackets) and head notes (in *italics*) are used when the sense of journal entries is doubtful or when allusions are obscure. Also names of places and persons are identified in footnotes.

I embarked on this project out of foolhardiness. Had I known the amount of work and agony editing a Journal such as this entailed, I probably would not have undertaken it. It was necessary to make two summer-trips to Sierra Leone, to work on the only extant copy at the Fourah Bay College. Decoding Ross' extremely fine handwriting after nearly 200 years where the ink had become faint was gruelling at times, but this was offset by the eventual pleasure of deciphering. It was also necessary to make two trips to London to rummage through some of the archives there to clarify some of Ross' obscure allusions.

My second trip to Africa landed me with what my doctor diagnosed as 'African fever,' and in editing the Journal in this state I found that I developed a feverish empathy with Ross who also suffered from 'the fever,' transmitting this to his Journal constantly while in Sierra Leone.

I am indebted to many for the completion of this Journal: to Mrs. Sheriff, head of the Fourah Bay Library and Archives, University of Sierra Leone, who most generously allowed me the use of a private room with special light and other facilities in her library, while editing this work which taxed one's sight; to Dominique of the Archives whose cheerful assistance was unflagging even when my demands for documents must have seemed unceasing; to J.R. Jarrett-Yaskey, head architect, Ministry of Works, Sierra Leone, without whose technical assistance I would not have deciphered some of the documents; to the staff of the Public Record Office and the British Museum, London, whose efficient assistance we who have researched there regularly have come to take for granted — almost.

Then there is Christopher Fyfe of the University of Edinburgh, the only other soul who has read the entire Journal in its original state and therefore it seems meet to dedicate the work to him. It would be difficult to overestimate his assistance, both in terms of inspiration and encouragement and in terms of pointing out errors and omissions and for pointing out sources I might otherwise have missed. His help was as steadfast as his knowledge of West Africa History seems inexhaustible.

I am also grateful to Prosser Gilford, Professor of History, and former Dean of the Faculty, Amherst College, for his encouragement and for reading the introduction and making valuable suggestions. A special word too, for those Amherst College students (and one from

Harvard) who assisted with the typing of the very first draft of the manuscript. It was not only their patience with a demanding taskmaster, and with a difficult text that I found impressive. I was also gratified to see their interest in, their understanding and their enjoyment of the Journal, which could have proved obscure to them without the necessary background knowledge.

I should note that this manuscript was enthusiastically accepted for publication some years ago by the Sierra Leone University Press (then a branch of the Oxford University Press, with Eldred Jones as editor), but, unfortunately, financial constraints sent the press out of circulation.

Mavis C. Campbell,
Department of History, Amherst College

NOTES

1. Sheldon H. Harris, *Paul Cuffe: Black America and the African Return* (New York: Simon and Schuster, 1972), p. 73.

2. For a comprehensive history of the Maroons of Jamaica, see Mavis C. Campbell, *The Maroons of Jamaica, 1655-1796: A History of Resistance, Collaboration and Betrayal* (Massachusetts: Bergin and Garvey, 1988),

3. For a study of the Maroons in Nova Scotia, see Mavis C. Campbell, *Nova Scotia and the Fighting Maroons: A documentary History* (Williamsburg: College of William and Mary Press, Studies in Third World Societies, 1990).

4. Paul Leicester Ford, ed., *The writings of Thomas Jefferson, 1807-1815*, Vol. IX (New York: G.P. Putnam's Sons, 1899), pp. 303-304.

5. Ibid.

6. See, for instance, James Theodore Holly and J. Dennis Harris, *Black Separation and the Caribbean, 1860* (Ann Arbor: The University of Michigan Press, 1970); also, P.J. Staudenraus, *The African Colonization Movement, 1816-1865* (New York: Columbia University Press, 1961) among others.

7. Folarin Shyllon, *Black People in Britain*, 1555-1833 (London: New York, Ibadan: Oxford University Press, 1977), P. 102. The disparity is in part due to the fact that their population fluctuated from time to time.

8. Ibid., p. 103.

9. Ibid.

10. Ibid., pp. 104-5

11. Ibid., p. 121.

12. Ibid., p. 124.

13. Ibid., p.146, who said 441, and in defending it, gave Parliamentary Papers (1789 Vol. 82 as his source in n. 43 on p.149, while Christopher Fyfe, *A History of Sierra Leone* (Oxford: The Clarendon Press, 1968), p. 19, said 4ll. Fyfe maintained that after subtracting deaths and runaways, 411 finally sailed. Letter from Fyfe to author, September 15, 1979.

14. Folarin Shyllon, *Black People*, p.132.

15. Christopher Fyfe, *History*, p.21. How did the Black Poor respond to the scheme? Suspicious at first, they were soon won over by a friend of Sharp's, but again, at the final stage of the plans, unsavory rumors about Sierra Leone excited this distrust. Among the rumors was that which said that the blacks would become victims of the slave traders on the West Coast of Africa. Frightened, some went into hiding and the authorities practically forced others on board. Those who finally went first asked for 'papers' to show that they were free persons. Thus they were issued by the navy, certificates bearing the Royal Arms. Such documents allegedly gave them the status of free citizens of 'the Colony of Sierra Leone or the Land of Freedom.' But whether these documents had any effect at all once in Sierra Leone, unfortunately has not been made clear.

16. For an account of the short-lived 'Province of Freedom,' see Ibid., pp.19-25. See also John Peterson, *Province of Freedom* (Evanston: Northwestern University Press, 1969), pp. 17-27.

17. Ford, *Thomas Jefferson*, p.303.

18. An Account of the Colony of Sierra Leone (Report of the Board of Directors. London:James Phillips, 1795), pp.107-108.

19. Ibid.

20. For a good account of these recaptives in Africa and elsewhere, see Monica Schuler, *Alas, Alas, Kongo*...(Baltimore: John Hopkins Press, 1980), *Passim*.

21. Ford, *Thomas Jefferson*, p.303.

22. Robert Thorpe, *A letter to William Wilberforce...Vice President of the African*

Institution, containing Remarks on the Sierra Leone Company...(London: E.C.&J. Rivington, 1805), p.41.

23. C.O. 217/70, Thornton to King, March 11, 1799.

24. Ibid.

25. See, among others, Lamont D. Thomas, *Rise to Be a People: A Biography of Paul Cuffe* (Urbana and Chicago:University of Illinois Press, 1986), pp.32-35 and *passim*.

26. Christopher Fyfe, *Sierra Leone Inheritance*(London: Oxford University Press, 1964), p.109.

27. Ibid., pp.109 and 111.

28. Thomas Fowell Buxton, *The African Slave Trade and its Remedy*(London: John Murray Publishers, 1839), p.12.

29. C.O 217/73, Portland to Wentworth, January (n.d.) 1800. See also W.O. 1/352, Portland to chairman of Sierra Leone Company, March 5, 1799.

30. C.O. 267/24, Thompson to Castlereagh, November 2, 1808.

31. Ibid.

32. Harris, *Paul Cuffe*, p.13.

33. Ibid., p.191

34. Thomas, *Paul Cuffe*, pp.50-71.

35. Harris, *Paul Cuffe*, pp.83-85.

36. Ibid. and Thomas, *Paul Cuffe*, pp.51-52.

37. *Substance of the Report of the Sierra Leone Company* (London: George Yard, Lombard Street, 1801), p.23.

38. R.S. Rattary, *Ashanti* (Oxford:The Clarendon Press, 1969), p.135.

39. R.C. Dallas, *The History of the Maroons*...(London:T.N. Longman and O. Rees, 1803), p.136.

40. For further accounts on Montague James and the 1795 Maroon war see Campbell, *The Maroons of Jamaica*, chap. 7. But for a complete biography of him, see Campbell , "Early Resistance to Colonialism..." in J.F. Ade Ajayi and J.D.Y. Peel, eds. *People and Empires in African History*... (London and New York: Longman), 1992.

41. Council Meeting, Sierra Leone, March 26, 1801.

42. Ibid., June 2, 1801.

43. It is reasonably certain that the urbane and mature architect, J.R. Jarrett-Yaskey, Professional Head, Ministry of Works, Sierra Leone, whose assistance to this author in her research has been unstinting, can claim Major Jarrett as one of his forebears.

44. C.O. 217/70, wentworth to John King, August 18, 1799.

45. Christopher Fyfe, *History*, pp.188-189.

46. Arthur T. Porter, *Creoledom: A Study of the Development of Freetown Society* (London: Oxford University Press, 1963), p.14.

47. Christopher Fyfe to author, April 9, 1978; from Zachary Macaulay's unpublished 'Notes.' This must have happened soon after Ross was appointed to the Sierra Leone Company, in December 1795, when he took up his appointment in January the following year.

48. Council Meetings, Sierra Leone, August 24 & 26, 1797.

THE JOURNAL

Ross' detailed and lengthy account of peculation connected with Maroon provisions at the very beginning of the Journal - in mid-Atlantic - may seem trivial from the hindsight of time. But the question of provisions was of immense importance by the then standards of marine practices. Again, the very cloistered nature of sea travel would tend to inflate the importance of just about any occurrence on board.

The Maroons were defrauded of some of their bread and some of their provisions were actually sold for profits in Halifax even before they left Nova Scotia. Their rum, too, was diluted with water and this rankled with the old Maroons, accustomed as they were to the full-spirited Jamaican rum. The British Lieutenant, John Sheriff, who was in command of the Asia transport was also responsible for Maroon provisions, and apparently he was somewhat connected with the fraud - either from poor supervision of from collusion with his steward, Jarrett.

Led by Colonel Montague James, the Maroons complained to Sheriff, who prevaricated initially. But after great pressure was brought to bear upon him by George Ross himself, Captain Smith of the Maroons, and Lieutenant Lionel Smith, Sheriff finally admitted that after being ignorant of any fraud at first, he soon became aware of it. But apparently he took no action. Finally Jarrett, the steward, was removed in disgrace and Captain Smith replaced him and things went well thereafter.

Sheriff's behaviour may be compared with that of another agent, Joseph Irwin, who also was in charge of provisions for another group of blacks, the Black Poor of England, bound also for Sierra Leone (1787). This group equally suffered from short supplies, perhaps more acutely than the Maroons, and Irwin was charged with short-changing their provisions, which he denied. Olaudah Equiano or Gustavus Vassa, mentioned above, who was made Commissary to the Black Poor by the British government, was vociferous in his condemnation of Irwin, but this soon brought about Vassa's dismissal as Commissary, Irwin having had friends in high places in London.[1]

Lieutenant Lionel Smith, of the Twenty-fourth regiment of Foot, commanded on board the Asia, 45 British troops on their way home on sick leave. But having his own charge did not prevent him from becoming actively supportive of the Maroons' claims. He relentlessly took issue with Sheriff

*until the latter finally admitted that he was aware of the short supplies. Smith
soon gained the respect and trust of the Maroons who demonstrated this by
having him appointed their agent for prize money accruing to them when, en
route, they captured a Spanish ship.*

*There are many Smiths to be encountered in this Journal. To prevent con-
fusion each is explained in footnotes. But Captain Smith - A Maroon - and
Lieutenant Smith, a British soldier, whom Ross addresses always by his sur-
name only, are the two Smiths, most mentioned, throughout the Journal. To
make for identification, upon every new introduction in the entries, the title,
'Captain' or 'Lieutenant' will be affixed.*

1800

✌ TUESDAY 9TH SEPTEMBER.

I took an opportunity this morning of seeing Captain Smith[2] and
Palmer,[3] and I told Smith that I had got the General[4] to promise to
speak to Sheriff[5] about letting them attend at the issuing out of provisions. I likewise suggested to him that in case Sheriff consented, he
might, when desired to attend, ask 'for what purpose?' And after the
answer to that question, he (Captain Smith), might, as occasion
served, introduce what he had told us last night - of this missing of
the spirits and pushing up the scale. By this means I expected to get
Sheriff acquainted with the proceedings of his Steward[6] - and if he
was not up to it already, I thought he certainly would take notice of
it.

While we were at breakfast, the General came in and asked Sheriff
to allow Captain Smith and Libert[7] to attend with Jarrett[8] to see the
Maroons' allowance issued out. Sheriff grunted and said he would -
might attend. The General went to inform them (Captain Smith and
Libert), and by and by came back with Smith - but in the interval the
General was gone, a few words took place between Sheriff, Lieu.
Smith[9] and myself which I think it proper to note. Some remark was
made by Sheriff on the General's message and I, in reply approved
of the message.

'What,' said Sheriff, 'do you suppose the Maroons are cheated of
their allowance?' 'Upon my word I do think so,' [said Ross.] 'You
think I stop their allowance - for what purpose should I stop their

allowance - what end could I have in doing it? Whatever provisions remain when they arrive at Sierra Leone shall be landed along with them,' (explained Sheriff.) I told him that I had not absolutely said that he did. But I had very good reason to believe it was done, and I further believed that his Steward of whom he always spoke so well, was no angel. I mentioned to him Lawrence[10] and Libert returning to my cabin yesterday after their allowance had been completed, and with joy in their faces saying, 'do you think if we been get this allowance we make a complain'? - and so on. 'Why don't they complain to me' (asked Sheriff) 'that man never complained to me - I am here to see that they have their fair allowance and if they think they don't receive that, why don't they let me know it'?

Lieu. Smith said that his people had been cheated out of part of their allowance upon which Sheriff complained that he was not told. 'No,' said Smith, 'I have of late heard so many fruitless complaints made to you that I did not think it worth my while, but you may be assured I shall take notice of it.' 'You may do as you will,' (said Sheriff.)

This conversation between Sheriff and Lieutenant Smith was more full and more pointed than I have here related it; in the course of it I recollect Smith's saying that upon his soul, he was sure the Maroons had been greatly cheated, and at another time he observed that his soldiers would have been greater sufferers were they as ignorant - that is, had they known as little about King's allowance as the poor unfortunate Maroons.

When Captain Smith came in, he asked Sheriff what it was intended he should do with the Steward and was informed that he should attend to the issuing out of the provision for the Maroons. But Smith said that he wished to be well informed of the business he was going upon, because if once he undertook it, he would like to carry it through in a proper manner. For example, 'What orders has the steward about the Rum for the Maroons'? asked Smith. 'I have seen him mix water with it,' (but) Sheriff pretended ignoramus. Smith persisted; still he pretended ignoramus. I told him that the Maroons had had grog given them for Rum. Smith asked him (Sheriff) if those were his orders. 'No,' says he, 'I never gave any orders that the Maroons should have water mixed with their Rum, but if they would have it so they might.' 'Oh no Massa,' says Smith, 'they not have it so but the Steward, he make it so.' (Upon this Smith apparently left to see about the provision).

In the course of the forenoon we [Ross and Lieutenant Smith] took down an affirmation of Joseph Schuman, a soldier who had assisted the Steward - it goes to prove many frauds committed in the Gun Room as well as the selling of Kings provisions in Halifax.

Before Lieu. Smith left my cabin, Captain Smith came in. He had been at the issuing out of the provisions, where it seems Jarrett's attendance was dispensed with by the Maroons. He (Captain Smith) brought about a quarter of a pound of bread in a handerchief which he said he had to take out of his own bread to make up yesterday's weight of Lawrence's. He however, told us that there was a general rejoicing among the Maroons - that it was agreed on all hands they never had so much allowance as today.

We already congratulated each other on our victory obtained over so much Iniquity - and told Captain Smith by no means to check the honest joy of the Maroons, but on the contrary that we should have no objection to seeing a deputation from them to thank Lieu. Sheriff for allowing him (Captain Smith) to attend them today, as their allowance was today much more ample than heretofore.

After dinner, before we had left the Mess Room, in comes the General, Johnson, Baily, Gray and Smith [all Maroons] and the General gave many hundred grandy tanks[11] to Sheriff, telling him that the Maroons were all happy today, that they had got a good allowance, and that had they always got the same, they never would complain. Sheriff was glad; hoped they would have no more cause of complaint, and took care to inform them that the manner in which Lawrence's mess came to be short yesterday was that a quantity of his bread had, in being delivered, fallen down in the 'tween decks, and that Jarrett had picked it up today - a pound and a half, he called it, but Jarrett will tell them about it.

The Maroons left us, and presently it was remarked - I believe by myself - that now it appeared plain beyond a doubt that the Maroons had been defrauded. Sheriff said that if it was so, he had known nothing at all of it. We all thought the very broad hints we had from time to time given him - and indeed the more that hints -the plain language (in which) we had told him today, as well as the daily cries of Misery from the Maroons were sufficient intimation to him. But he said he was sure he had given orders that their fair allowance should be issued, and if it had not been done, it was none of his fault; he had done his duty. I was surprised, I told him, at his apparent indifference upon witnessing the fraud about to be committed on poor Lawrence and his Mess. 'How do you know,' said he, (Sheriff) 'what I may have done in consequence of that'? I know what you said and did while myself was present, and circumstances enable me to form a pretty correct opinion what you have done since you have attempted to put us and the Maroon officers off with that flimsy excuse of Jarrett's which no one but yourself would have given the least countenance to.' 'Do you suppose I invented it?' (asked Sheriff) 'No, but I'm well assured it is an invention to cover a fraud - and if Jarrett is called in now it must certainly appear so.'

Jarrett the steward, Montague, Smith and O'Connor's wife were called in; (the Steward's countenance was a most miserable sight, and he rested [?] outside the window, near by his Patron) (Sheriff).

[Apparently Ross now proceeded to question Jarrett]

'Jarrett, how much bread did you pick up in the 'tween decks yesterday?'

J. 'Oh a great deal Massa'

Q. I daresay as much as two pounds-out of whose mess did this fall? - heigh?

J. 'I don know; it fall all day'

Q. 'Do two pounds fall in the course of every day's issue? Heigh?'

J. 'I don know'

Q. 'Did you ever see such a quantity before'?

J. 'I never did.'

Q. 'Did any fall out of it?'

J. 'I don know, I suppose some fall out of it'

Q. 'You were there to see that the Maroons had their fair allowance. Could one pound have fallen out of three without your seeing it?'

J. Did not think so.

Q. 'Did two pounds fall in the issue of one day while you were placed there by the Maroons to watch over their allowance - and did you not see it?'

- he supposed some of it might have fallen before yesterday. However O'Connor's wife, who, it seems, lives below in the Orlop Deck, and the daily recourse to the place they call the "tween decks said positively that she had yesterday picked up all the bread in that place and it only amounted to two or three little pieces - whereas the making up of Lawrence's took (actually) 5 large Biscuits whole and several pieces.

There followed a pretty severe exposure of Jarrett's conduct -his only excuse was that he did not understand the weights. But he muttered and threatened a good deal, particularly relative to the time he once landed - that he had but one life to lose and so on.[12]

After this when the Maroons had left, a very smart conversation took place between Sheriff and Lieu. Smith in the course of which Smith told him plainly that if he did not exert himself during the remainder of the passage in seeing justice done to the Maroons he would assuredly have him brought to a court martial. 'You may do as you like' (Sheriff replied), and later observed to Lieu. Smith that he had no business to interfere; he had nothing at all to do in it. But Smith's reply was that as a King's officer he would not see his provisions squandered away -and as a man he dared to support the cause of humanity - and he would not see the Maroons in future treated as they had been without bringing him to a severe account for it. Sheriff set him at defiance; he said he knew his Instructions and had acted up to them. Smith did not know what the Instructions were but he knew what his (Sheriff's) conduct had been.

They were very warm for a little but by and by they cooled and spoke somewhat more explanatory - Smith telling Sheriff very candidly the proofs he could produce of the Steward's guilt. [Ross now indulges in some reflective moments concerning Sheriff.] Now (did I think) Sheriff if you are a man - if you have a generous -an honorable or an honest sentiment within you - now, come forward-Confess that those frauds were committed without your knowledge -even confess Man that you were more remiss than you ought to have been - thank Smith for this trouble he has taken and by his assistance in setting matters as much as possible to rights; he will freely give it you (and so shall we all); he is this moment in a generous humour - you will be the best friends and our Mess shall go on pleasantly. But no; nothing of the kind from Sheriff - he still persisted in the same indecision, unaccountable and inexpressible kind of humour which he has all along indulged in.

In the course of the afternoon upon the solicitation of Captain Smith, Lieu. Smith allowed that Corporal Smith[13] should go to assist Captain Smith in making him acquainted with the weights etc. This Corporal Smith has only this afternoon been promoted from the ranks and N.B. Corporal or Secretary Hawkyand has been sent to do duty as a private soldier on account of his part in the villany practiced on board the *Asia*.

Oh true: I believe it was in the course of the conversation which took place immediately after the departure of the officers who came to return thanks, that Sheriff asked me whether I did not remember the paragraph in the letter I delivered him from the Transport Board which stated that I was to act jointly with him in the management of the Maroons on the passage. I said I remembered his having read over that letter to me and could likewise recollect a paragraph similar to that he mentioned. It was immediately either before or after this that he said he was determined to set on foot an enquiry into his conduct on Board, as he deemed it requisite for the clearing of his character.

[An exasperating habit of Ross, is to introduce a trend of thought or a subject out of the blue without any apparent connection whatsoever, as seen in his very next sentence.] How ridiculous he looked seeing that boy flogged.[14] In the course of a conversation I had with Montague in the evening he told me that he had long enough ago complained to Mr. Sheriff about the Maroons' getting grog instead of rum.

∾ WEDNESDAY 10TH SEPTEMBER.

Elsy Jarrett[15] is delivered of a son today - the father of it is Charles Shaw.[16] It seems this young adventurer has come forth before his time, and Jarrett[17] vows if the child should die before he is an old man, Barnet must be brought to justice for it.

Be it known to all whom it may concern that in the first place I was present with Mr. Chamberlain[18] in Preston when Elsy Jarrett made her first complaint against Barnet and it was on this very identical day he had given her the thumping.

Item. I was present, and particularly called upon by Mr. Chamberlain to witness to it. That certain two Maroons who were then present in the Hunk [?] Hull[?] but whom I at present cannot charge my memory with (tho' I think they were Montague and Major Baily) made their appearance there before Mr. Chamberlain telling him that whereas they had become Bail for the appearance of the said Barnet in case any injury befel the said Elsy within a certain limited span, and whereas the said limited span had now expired and the said Elsy had perfectly recovered and was in perfect health -they had therefore presented themselves there to have all responsibility taken off them, on account of the said bail they had entered into.

Satan has, it seems, been kicking up a dust today because Sheriff won't give her a bottle of rum for every birth she brings to light: [about 6 lines omitted; not intelligible]. Latitude today 28.4, breezy.

✂ *Thursday 11th September*

Latitude 26.12. I was busy writing in my Cabin all this morning - 'hallo Smith: What, armed at dinner - how comes this?' (Lieu. Smith)

As he was in danger of having his throat cut he was determined not to submit with philosophical calmness to the operation. It seems he has been getting one of his men flogged today, and a sailor on the poop hollowed out loudly - 'Oh shame - shame by G.D.' Upon making an enquiry into this, Smith thought he discovered a disposition in the sailor to insult him etc. etc., and so clapt on a Bayonet to his Breech.

After dinner, a conversation started by Sheriff, took place between himself and Lieu. Smith. In the course of it Sheriff complained that his situation on board was unpleasant, wished it were otherwise; and so did Smith. But he (Smith) observed that at present there were certain impediments to be removed before this could be. Sheriff did not know what they were. Smith repeated the old story, observing or rather commenting upon the cool indifference with which Sheriff seemed to have taken every thing said to him lately. Sheriff said he had not been quite so indifferent as he (Smith) imagined: he now told us of some active steps he had taken in regard to the Steward, and made such a declaration as I am sure made us all happy. It amounted to this: that he was well convinced of the fraud carried on but that till very lately, he had *been perfectly ignorant of them*. I feel particularly rejoiced and relieved at hearing this and said so. I also said that I, at the same time, felt indignant at the reception our well meant officers met with from Sheriff - by which it appeared that he made light of our feelings for him and for the cause of humanity. After a good deal of Explanatory conversation between Sheriff and Smith (which as I trust Sheriff is still an honest man, I need not be so particular about), it was agreed the Steward should be called in, arrested, and discharged from the store-room and put in confinement.

Sheriff said that from a calculation he had made yesterday it appeared that there was at present a week's allowance of beef to the whole ship on board more than there ought to be - and we are not as yet five weeks from Halifax: pretty savings: pretty pickings:

Indeed, poor unfortunate Maroons - if you did complain, it plainly appears you complained *not* without cause.

⋘ FRIDAY 12TH SEPTEMBER.

Fine Trade passing the Atlantic, but on account of the state of the ship no sport was allowed today. Latitude at noon 23.44. Poor Smith! (Lieu.) Today he tells me some of his soldiers have been heard to ' threaten they would pop him off if ever we should (get) into action. No bad sport to hear us determine in case of an action to put some of the soldiers in the custody of the Maroons.

This day passed rather quietly and the Mess seems coming to a better understanding. I find after all Sheriff will have a touch at the Cape-de Verde.[19] How Palmer[20] bothered us today about letting him have a Horse and Goat, etc. etc.

⋘ SATURDAY 13TH SEPTEMBER.

Fine Trade still. Latitude 21.24 - but hang it all -how could we have got the ship in the Longitude of 36 West - that is certainly too bad with a fair wind all the way from St. Marys[21] to the Cape de Verde. [about three lines omitted; unintelligible]

⋘ SUNDAY 14TH SEPTEMBER.

No prayers today. Latitude 18.44. Had a great many scholars. Sam Stone's wife has brought in a girl today. Had a chat in the forenoon with the General, Johnson, and Palmer about Sierra Leone and made them very happy.

⋘ MONDAY 15TH SEPTEMBER.

St. Nicholas[22] in sight in the morning. It has a very remarkable appearance from the North and Easterly but I cannot either describe or delineate it. We left St. Nicholas on our right hand and stowed away direct for St. Jago[23] - but it was very hazy all day and not too much wind.

⋘ TUESDAY 16TH SEPTEMBER.

Nasty wet morning and no wind. By and by a breeze sprung up and we got sight of St. Jago. Sheriff supposed it to be Mayo, but from its size we afterwards determined it to be St. Jago.

The wind freshened with now and then some rain but it blowed right off the island - how peculiarly unfortunate we are when we attempt making any land.

At 10 A.M. saw a large ship standing for us from the North end of the island. We got all ready for action. She first showed Portuguese colours, but presently hauled them down and sported an English Ensign with a long pendant at her mast head. She proved to be the *Arthuran Frigate*, Captain woolly,[24] five weeks from England bound to St. Helena. She had been two days beating about here attempting to make the island. After she had sent a Lieutenant on board of us, and picked up our news, she stowed for the island but still the wind is right foul.

∾ WEDNESDAY 17TH SEPTEMBER.

Great was my surprise this morning to find both ourselves and the Frigate to the eastward of Mayo. We had very, very nigh got on shore the Reefs - north east end of Mayo. The wind came north easterly again and we stood away large for St. Jago. Came to an Anchor about 3 o'clock in 15 fathom water just as we were coming in to the Bay it fell calm and our situation was for half an hour very unpleasant at the mercy of a nasty cross current fish or something and at no distance from the Rock - and to add to our comfort no soundings for a moderate line.

This Bay I find a very bad and unsafe Roadstead from July or August to February or March. It is during the months between August and March they have the kind of Winter or Rains there is here - and at that time the regular Trade Wind is continually interrupted by calms and South West Winds, for I apprehend they have the rains here generally from the West or South West.

So dangerous is it riding in Praya Bay with a South West Wind that, in coming in today, we saw two Vessels beating up for the Harbour, having a few nights ago been obliged on the setting of the S. West breeze to cut their cables and put to sea.

Sheriff went on board the *Arethusa* and brought in the acceptable intelligence that Goree has lately been taken by two English Frigates.

The *Arethusa* is but 3 weeks from England.

We went on shore in the evening and had to land on the Beach with an ugly surf - for there is nothing here in (the) nature of a wharf or landing place. Here there is a kind of Fort and a Regiment of Soldiers but - miserable is the appearance they make.

We bought a few oranges and lemons and guavas at about half a dollar a hundred.

It was perfectly in character to see Captain Woolly with the greatest coolness and *sang froid* sucking away at an orange, while that

Tinsell'd all over Gentleman, the Governor's secretary, was enquiring of him about the European news with a long solemn countenance as tho' the fate of Nations depended on it - and at the same time his hat in hand and a low weary nod of Woolly's. In short, the contrast was entertainingly striking and, and I said before, in character.

ᥱ THURSDAY 18TH SEPTEMBER.

Went on shore about 11 o'clock to purchase some fruit as Sheriff [is] determined to sail in the afternoon. The *Arethusa* has, it seems, already lost an anchor and our bottom is by no means safe. I laid out about 7 dollars more. When I came on board and counted, I had as follows: 550 oranges, 96 coconuts, 110 guavas, 2 bunches of bananas - small bunches, 2 papaws, a bunch of garlick, and some vine setts[?] - but I can with much safety say that [unclear] of 200 oranges and 50 guavas, 50 coconuts etc. etc., I went below into my cabin to distribute a few presents among the Maroons.

While the bay was gone, from time to time my ears could not help receiving the sound of mutiny from the Captain's Cabin adjoining. It was the Boatswain's voice and there were besides, the voices of the Carpenter and Tracey the 2nd mate.

All the ship's motions and all the transactions on board of her were canvassed in form and with the greatest perspicacity. My job being finished, I went up, and of course mentioned what I had been hearing.

After supper, Sheriff, Lieu. Smith and myself went upon the Quarter Deck. Sheriff and I were looking out for the North Pole Star - a sailor (the Spaniard) was insultingly drunk. Sheriff thumped him forward - and not being able to silence him brought him aft again and was preparing to have him locked up in the rigging. I was at this moment standing with Smith on the opposite side of the quarter Deck. I had observed when Sheriff was bringing the man aft to seize him, (that) the Boatswain whisper something to Tracy, who went below and returned again presently. At this moment, as I was saying, when I was standing with or near Smith on the larboard side of the Quarter Deck, the Boatswain had come and stood before us in a rather expressive position (or I thought [so]) looking intently over to Sheriff. Presently he clap'd his hand to his thigh and advanced two steps or three. I immediately whispered to Smith my suspicion that it was a Pistol [that] made the noise I heard when he applied his hand to his breech. Smith said he believed I was right, and he had thought the same, and presently he calls up all his Men under Arms and ranged them on the Poop and Quarter Deck.

The drunken Sailor was seized up and kept there for perhaps 3 qrs. of an hour, in the course of which time he uttered several expressions respecting the transactions [made with?] the ship which certainly were never his original ideas.

Among others [other questions?] he asked Sheriff to tell him what business the ship had into St. Jago. And further, among others, he after abusing Smith most lustily said 'he was waiting to take his life' (sic). But the vagabond was very drunk, and made no more noise after he had a very hearty vomiting.

We went to bed about 12 o'clock - Smith thought proper to keep his men under arms all night.

I gave the hint to Captain Smith of the Maroons, and told him if he heard a Pistol go off, it was the alarm and he was to rouse the Maroons instantly and repair to Lieu. Smith's cabin, and mine for arms.

We got under way from St. Jago about 4 o'clock in the afternoon and shaped a course for Brava but it fell almost dead calm in the course of the evening.

A French privateer Brig lately cut out of this Bay an English south Sea Man and returned to land her people. Do you ask how the Portuguese allowed all this? They will tell you that the 'Frenchman threatened to take the island:'

༄ *FRIDAY 19TH SEPTEMBER.*

I find Smith [obviously, Lieutenant Smith] did not go to bed all last night. We make but a very poor first of it for Brava - beginning of the day calm and the afternoon, a foul wind and ahead for Brava, and fair for Sierra Leone, and the appearance of a dirty night - it was resolved at 8 in the evening to bear away for Sierra Leone direct - which was accordingly done. So good bye Brava: tho' much I wished to see thee - I am a son of Adam, and what son of the Old Man but must bend to circumstances?

༄ *SATURDAY 20TH SEPTEMBER.*

After a nasty squall last night it fell calm about 11 o'clock and continued so all night, and this morning we found ourselves at no great distance, to the Southward from Togo[25] - air thick but saw St. Jago, Brava and Togo.

In the afternoon a very young trade breeze sprung up. I was busy today putting away the things I had loosed out for the Brava market and setting my cabin a little to rights again - I allowed Captain Smith to sell some of the things to such of the Maroons as wanted them.

℘ SEPTEMBER 20 AND 1ST JAY[?] SUNDAY 21ST SEPTEMBER.

A nice 6 or 7 knot Trade Breeze - bravo! A ship in sight standing to the southward, supposed to be the *American* we left in St. Jago bound to the River Plate. No progress today not a word about them. I had a few scholars - about a dozen or so.

℘ MONDAY 22ND SEPTEMBER.

The Breeze is but very small. I begin to fear the Trade is upon his last legs. We had shocking bad weather today. Things seem to have gone on more quietly on board within the last two or three days. I believe the troublesome Lads begin to feel a little cow'd.

℘ TUESDAY 23RD SEPTEMBER.

Breeze still exists but is very slender. Lat. 10.37.

℘ WEDNESDAY 24TH SEPTEMBER.

Still exists the Breeze. Lat. 9.38. It was today I begin writing my B.[?]

℘ THURSDAY 25TH SEPTEMBER.

The Breeze had his Breathing stopped by two or three showers about noon today - he's dead, I daresay. Lat. 9.4, Long. supposed about 20.
Saw a Sail today standing to the Southward. Gave Captain Smith a Bottle of Port Wine.

℘ FRIDAY 26TH SEPTEMBER.

Oh yes: It was most true that the Trade died yesterday. After he had made his exit, we in the afternoon had a little breeze sprung up more to the Southward and Eastward - but that soon died away and we were becalmed all night.
Blow heavily Breeze blow - and let us have a look how they come on to Sierra Leone once more.
Swarms of Swallows hovering about our ship these 2 or 3 days.

∾ Saturday 27th September.

Calms and light North easterly. A Bottle of [not intelligible] to the Mess.

∾ Sunday 28th September.

A nice northerly breeze all the morning - but cloudy.

Saw banks of fog or something ahead. I don't suppose there was a Soul who saw it but took it for land - but it was no land. Lat. 8.20. Becalmed from 12 to 6 then sprung a little breeze -from the Southward with small drizzling rain.

∾ Monday 29th September.

It was a nasty night. Some squalls and calms but a great deal or rain. Sounded three times but no bottom. A great deal of rain today but towards evening got sight of the Cape and the Bananas[26] - Cape about ESE.

ARRIVAL IN SIERRA LEONE

[This might have been just another entry to Ross, but it was a momentous occasion to the Maroons who were returning to their ancestral home.]

∾ Tuesday 30th September.

Last night we lay off and expecting to get in this morning - but the morning it fell calm and so it continued till 3pm.

A breeze then sprung up and we came to an anchor a little below the settlement at 8 o'clock.

Sheriff seemed to place much confidence in his chart - I think it very ill deserved; it directed him to get the Peak of Lyon Loaf SSW of him and then stand boldly in - and it told him he should be in soundings before he could see the Land. I only can say to the last - that at 8 in the morning of the 29th there was no bottom at 70 fathoms and I am very sure that with a clear day we should before that have made the land. I suppose between that time and 3p.m. we might have gone about 12 miles or so and at 3, we sounded in 15 fathoms.

Cox[27] came on board just before we came to an anchor and told us the Colony was in a state of Insurrection[28] and was glad to see us. I went on shore with him.

We called on Mr. Gray[29] on our way and Fothingill.[30] At the Govt. House we saw Gov. Ludlam[31] no - don't! Wilson, Macauly[32] MacMillan,[33] Bright [34] and Pickering [35] and one Viner[36] - all in arms - Guards mounted, etc.

The Settlement is certainly improving fast in point of health - I wish my Face[?] may say the same 3 years after this.

Sheriff having come to an Anchor came up a while after and having delivered our several credentials walked on Board.

‿ WEDNESDAY 1ST OCTOBER.

Lieu. Smith and myself breakfasted at the Gov. House. I did not like Ludlaw's method of asking people for their opinions - flying from one to another. Why not bring us together and let all our sentiments be known to all - this looks too much like Mr. Macaulay's inquisitorial system. I find Lieu, Smith got him to consent to the adopting of prompt and decisive measures and I'm glad of it:

From the state in which I find the settlement I almost instantaneously last night changed from every idea I had formerly entertained in regard to the place the Maroons should be settled in - and recommended - or at least suggested as strongly as I could the settling them back of the present settlers on this side of the water.

It seems land has been purchased and some buildings knocked up for them on the Bullom's side and Ludlam hammered much on the expense which should on that account be thrown away should the Maroons, after all, be settled on this side.

I, however, this morning, begged Lieu. Smith, if on acquainting himself with the circumstances he should be of the same mind with me to urge it. - Indeed, our Sentiments almost always hit it.

So by Noon between us we got Ludlam to admit that the Mountains this side of the water should be the spot destined for the Maroons.

Lieu. Smith went on board for his men and I accompanied him, for a few Maroon officers to introduce to the Governor - Gray and Cox came on board with us.

I had them both in my Cabin when I introduced the officers -told them I wanted a few of them to wait upon the Governor and asked whether it would be agreeable to them that old Jarrett should make one of their numbers - it was determined not.

I then introduced the unpleasant state of the Colony - my regrets on their account that it should be so - and appealed however to the candid manner in which I made all my representations to them.

It was astonishing to see how they received these tidings. Not a frown nor anything like it - but a cheerful countenance and repetitions of their assurances that the greatest candour had always been shown them and that the greatest fairness was intended them.

When they broke up, Gray and Cox could not find words to express their admiration at this specimen of the Maroons - far exceeding all beliefs, etc., etc.

I had Montague, Johnson, Baily, Smith, Palmer and Charles Shaw introduced to the Governor (Ludlam).

He made a speech to them - but kept looking on the ground and never looked any of them in the face all the while. This was shocking - particularly to Maroons who so much admire everything that is open and has a Manly appearance. His speech was very long - giving a circumstantial account of - but why say what? - for I'm sure they only knew of it that it was a repetition of what I had been telling them. Montague answered to his speech - that the country they had left had been too cold for them - that made them leave it. They had come here not for sunny [?] sorry [?] but for good - they like King George and white Man well - if them settler don't like King George nor this Government - only let Maroon see them.[37]

In short, from what I had told them previous to their coming on shore, they were well prepared to receive this speech and Captain Smith also answered to it - but his answer was a kind of explanatory repetition of what Montague had said.

The Governor then read over the Terms [38] to them and they agreed to them as when in Halifax.

In regard to the Article for Provision (7th Art.) I mentioned the terms in which I had explained it, viz., that without [unless] there was some previous fault on their parts, the Governor and Council never would entirely cut off their allowance till they could first point out to them the manner in which they could support themselves. The Governor agreed to this - and added that it might be reasonably expected that this condition would naturally fall to the ground, in the span of 12 months from this day.

There was a trifling alteration made in (the) 2nd article to please Baily, who, I am sorry to say it, was the worse of [for?] liquor. It was for the good of the Settlement' - and so passed the Terms.

Palmer and Shaw presently after whispered (to) me that there were two women who seemed not to like the country - that they did not know whether they should have mentioned them. 'Certainly not,'

[apparently, was Ross's reply.]

The evening was spent in a humdrumish way arranging matters for a general attack on the Rioters. The precaution being first used of sending a proclamation to them by Zimiri Armstrong[39] that without [unless] they came in by 10 in the evening or sent some proper persons to treat for them, all further dallying would be at an end.

It was past 10 when Zimiri came back with an answer that in the time given they could not see some of their principal persons but that the *terms* pleased them well and they would be in in the morning.

It was, I suppose, near midnight when the plan of attack was finally arranged. It was this, viz:

Sheriff and Macaulay were to go by water with a party of 40 Maroons to Thompson's Bay. I, with 30 Maroons was to go up by my own farm and fall down the opposite side of the mountain upon the Lots of Cowper and Laurie White, while I detach Palmer with about 15 Maroons in an Easterly direction and Tolley with 15 Maroons was to guard the pass below Washington. We went on board to get the Maroons in readiness and landed about 60 of them. We had hardly landed when it blew a violent Tornado - unfortunate.

It seems no use reciting the difficulties we experienced and the much greater we had narrowly escaped inlanding - as well as the peculiar obstinacy of Sheriff.

When we got on the hill the Tornado set the idea of making the attack that night out of the question with us, and we expected those on board might be of the same mind - or at least that they should not begin the attack until the signal was made which was to be 2 guns from the Fort at 5 o'clock.

For my own part I had a most precious fagging night of it -enough to knock up any poor vagabond.

☙ THURSDAY 2ND OCTOBER.

Contrary to our expectations Sheriff and Macaulay with their party proceeded up the River after the Tornado was over. They came to Thornton Hill about 8 o'clock this morning, they had a scuffle with a party of the Rascals, killed two, taken two prisoners, and supposed to have wounded some. Elliott and Anderson were the 2 killed.

The 70 Maroons on the Hill, besides Sheriff's party which had been out got in readiness and sallied forth at 9 o'clock in two parties under Lieu. Smith and myself in order to scour the country.

I, of course, allowed Smith to have his choice of the Maroons as well as to chuse his route. He went over the ground where the action had taken place in the morning and took several suspected persons whom he sent in prisoners. I only sent in 3 [or?] 10. My route lying up by Kizell's over Washington Hill up to and beyond Elliott's, down by Laurie White's and here by the bloody ground. I however got a good quantity of arms, that is, muskets, powder, shott, etc., etc. out of the Rebel's house. We both returned about 4 and all joined in praising the Maroons for a set of the finest Fellows and the best Bushmen ever was.

ᖉ *Friday 3rd October.*

This was a very rainy day but Sheriff and Macaulay with their party went up to the Governor's House.

A most unfortunate accident has happened: two Natives at work on the Governor's farm fled on sight of the Maroons - the Maroons consequently concluded they were game and fired and wounded them both. One expired of his wounds this evening - the other will recover with the loss of a hand.

ᖉ *Saturday 4th October.*

I made a sally this morning with 15 of my party but no face of a rebel was to be seen - we however got several more muskets etc.

It rained all the morning. Our route lay thro' my farm. I treated my people to as much Sugar Cane as they would. I was grieved to see my young coffees thrive so with -: -yes, I think I was. [sic].[40]

They are so choked up with weeds, and yet they do so well -that I was grieved at the thought - *what would those poor coffees be if they were taken care of?*

I find it is the same coffee as we had from St. Thomas, they are used to in Jamaica, for whenever we came to Gray's farm and saw a few of those plants, the Maroons were quite happy tho' they appeared perfectly unacquainted with the native Sierra Leone coffee - any more than knowing it to be coffee.

In the afternoon Pickering came on board with me. I went on shore again and was desired by the Governor to come up the Hill tomorrow to concert measures about the Maroons.

✤ SUNDAY 5TH OCTOBER.

We had prayers today at the Governor's House. Bright asked Clark to read over the *English Prayers* and MacMillan gave us (a) good allowance of old fashioned singing with the country hymns of some outlandish enthusiast - (he) read a sermon and made a prayer - after its kind.

It seemed agreed that Granville Town [41] is to be the situation of the Maroons. I made a calculation of the number of acres the Maroons would require agreeable with the terms and they amounted to 8 or 977 acres.

Determined to start with a party of the Maroons tomorrow to survey the mountains, and the Governonr expressed an intention of accompanying us as far as Granville Town.

✤ MONDAY 6TH OCTOBER.

Started from Thornton Hill with the Governor and a party of about 60 Maroons at 8 this morning - the old General at our head in top spirits.

After squandering two or three hours about Granville Town, the Governor, convoyed by his Guard, set out for Freetown and I, with 30 Maroons and Floyd for a guide - we went up the boundary line, or as nearly as we could guess so for 5 hours. A Tornado then came on and we made the best of our way under a pouring of rain to the Governor's House where we found Macaulay, Lieu. Smith and etc. who had come there in the morning with a party of Maroons upon information that Anderson and others skulked about there - but the information was proved to be false. I ate a most unmerciful supper and slept as sound as a stone till morning.

In the course of our journey thro' the mountain, the only thing worth noting that we saw was a number of fine coffee trees and plants.

✤ TUESDAY 7TH OCTOBER.

Returned in the morning to Town. Macaulay dined on board. For his own sake and Lieu. Smith's, I hope he may get the command of the *Asia*.

When I came home, I found a blaze lighted - as tho' the Maroons, impatient of the delay on board the ship insisted they should be landed immediately in Freetown and some had even taken houses there - this I thought would be a most prejudicial measure. I therefore, after consulting the Governor, went on Board, had a meeting of the Chiefs in my Cabin, and very easily persuaded them that it was their interest to put up with the present trifling inconveniences and set immediately about their own plans - that their sick should, that same evening be landed and all possible attention paid to them - and tomorrow a party of the Maroons should go to Granville Town to begin preparing for the whole [group?]. They were pleased, and I promised them further when they came then to give them a Dance - I could do no less.

The sick were landed accordingly and lodged in the church [which?].

✑ WEDNESDAY 8TH OCTOBER.

It was noon before I could get a Boat to land my party of 30 men and then we had to march up under the scorching sun to Granville Town.

Macarty's House was cleared out and part of the adjoining streets cut down[?]

I visited several of the Houses belonging to runaway rascals[42] in the neighbourhood of Granville Town accompanied by Captain Smith, Johnson, and Baily. Sheriff and Macaulay came up late with some stores and we all three returned overland with straw candles native fashion.

Bless my bonny eyes: What's this I see? Nothing less than 2 white Ladies in the Govt. House of Sierra Leone! Let me look -its Mrs. and Miss Bracey (wife and probably daughter of the Company's ship-wright). Oh - no great things, after all - but they're *white*.

✑ THURSDAY 9TH OCTOBER

Went to Granville Town today with an additional 20 and 3 women etc., etc. Sheriff had promised to come up and survey the Harbour but he humm'd and haw'd about it so that I was obliged to request the Governor to appoint Macaulay to do it. It was late before Macaulay came, so that little - very little has been done today with our 50 men.

✑ FRIDAY 10TH OCTOBER.

Went up in a Boat to Granville Town along with Macaulay, Gray and Hermitage. M. [Macaulay?] and I surveyed the rest of the Houses where we expect to quarter the Maroons. I got Elliott to give me a promise of his House till I could provide myself with mess and Mrs.? [not clear].

Returning in the evening by water, I just missed a Tornado by being in the *Asia* before it began!

❧ SATURDAY 11TH OCTOBER.

Walked up to Granville Town with a male party of Maroons today. Breakfasted there, returned at Noon. Robinson's examination going ıt Govt. House. I got a few words of [with?] the Governor and went back a second time to Granville Town and made it late before I returned.

Bought several things of MacMillan's for beginning housekeeping etc., etc.

Requested the Governor to order the *Asia* tomorrow to Granville Town Bay and he said he would.

❧ SUNDAY 12TH OCTOBER.

The Earl of Liverpool, Captain Harris, 28 days from Liverpool arrived today - brought a letter for the Governor and Council and a printed copy of the company's new charter.[43]

We had a laugh at the expense of the new appointments as they appeared: Thomas Cox, Mayor; George Ross, Alexander Smith and Thorne, Aldermen, and James Wilson, Sheriff.

Still hammering [?] about taking Macaulay in command of the *Asia*.

Willey in Town today - he puts up at Gray's - never, it seems, visits the governor.

The Asprey[?] Sloop of war with 50 soldiers and a ship with slaves[44] as well as materials for a Fort are now daily expected.

❧ MONDAY 13TH OCTOBER.

Waited on the Governor in the morning to request he would acquaint Sheriff if he recount (- ed) I should superintend the landing of the Maroons - Yes.

The *Asia* moved up to Granville Town. Nelly Sewell had a Fair tonight. Today, the Maroons had nothing to eat till very late in the afternoon. The poor creatures have truly been starved since they came into Port, and I never saw people bear hard usage better than they have uniformly done.

↶ TUESDAY 14TH OCTOBER.

Landed this morning with some of the officers and had a palaver on the best plan to adopt for making a speedy landing.

We found old Jarrett very noisy and troublesome - he wanted to go to live at Freetown. 'No'; he then said he never would live with the Maroons: 'Then write down your sentiments and let me lay them before the Governor and I'll answer for it, you shall be at liberty to go when you will out of their jurisdiction.' [replied Ross - apparently]. After breakfast, I went to visit some of the empty houses with him. I now and then lent him my gun to shoot and we were great friends.

Had a very bustling day of it indeed - but tho' I flagged much I had the satisfaction of thinking that I pleased and accommodated the poor and much persecuted Maroons.

Left the Asia today for good - thank God: [four or five words unintelligible] and they sent me a very handsome thank you sir![45]

My Liquor Case, wine and Brandy went all to the Dogs through the carelessness of Captain Palmer.

↶ WEDNESDAY 15TH OCTOBER.

First thing this morning again, Jarrett kicked up another dust - the troublesome vagabond: And the hotheaded blustering Rascal: What can be a man's motive for endeavouring to set peopole by the ears? - when he sees a disposition on all hands to accommodate and make matters agreeable. Because he fancied himself a little crop'd in not getting exactly the House he set his eye upon he got on [?] making such a noise and swore he never would build a House for himself so long as he lived. I heard him a long time and spoke to him sharper than I am used to do - but upon hearing the last expression I told him coolly I had heard enough -that I would certainly represent what he had said to the Governor and I had not a doubt but he should have his wish of yesterday -' to live distant from the Maroons.'

I, of course, said no more to him - but presently after, went to Montague and told him what I intended to do, but that I thought
it proper to let him know first. That old man said he would speak to the other officers and let me hear from him presently.

By and by, he called upon me to come where 3 or 4 officers and Jarrett were present. He told me Jarrett was on his repentance for what he had said. Jarrett pulled off his hat and begged ten thousand pardons and if ever I heard him talk so again I might cut his tongue out of his head. It was agreed that if I forgave Jarrett for this time he would go to live in the house D. Shaw had pitched upon for himself which Shaw resigned in his favour. After a very severe reprimand I patched the business up - I hardly know whether I was right in so doing - 'twere best we were rid of him -for he will be sure to break out again and again as long as he lives.

Poor Palmer's Dog: - And poor Palmer - after giving his poor Dog a part of his own allowance all the way from Nova Scotia to be the very first night after landing devoured by a ravenous leopard!!

∾ THURSDAY 16TH OCTOBER.

Had a walk this morning around all the houses of the Maroons settled in the country - seeing their situations, and taking down the order of their Misses.

When I came back, here was another row waiting me, set on foot, it seems by Nash Hamilton who laid claim to the house Captain Smith meant for himself. I was accused of partiality to Smith on the occasion - but most unjustly: for instead of my appointing Smith to the house, it was his desire to have it - and so strongly did he desire it too, that had I said more than I did say to dissuade him from it, he might accuse me of partiality on the other side of the question. After I had explained the matter to the General he was pleased - and seeing him satisfied I made him have Some chocolate with me. I esteem the old man for the desire he always shows to have right done - tho' I own it goes against my grain to hold forth explaining as tho' I was anxious to have myself justified to him.

Lieutenant Smith called after breakfast; Macaulay called in the evening to go to Town with me but as I could not get out of the store till past 8 p.m. he stayed with me all night and agreed we should start early in the morning. Received $50 of Pickering to Account.[46]

∾ FRIDAY 17TH OCTOBER.

Walked into Town with Macaulay. Dined on Thornton Hill - that is, breakfasted there - No - No! I had 9/ - to pay for a piece of Pork I had for Dinner, and had Hermitage and MacMillan to help me out with it - also the General.

The General complains much of heat - but the remembrance of the cold of Nova Scotia will ever be a sufficient check. The Maroons, would, I believe grumble not a little on account of the heat were this their first country after Jamaica.[47]

The Maroons had to go without their allowances today owing to the dilatory manner (in which) we get the provisions from our board - it has been invariably so since our first landing.

⋘ SATURDAY 18TH OCTOBER.

This morning, instead of letting us have sufficient provisions to issue a week's allowance, Sheriff sent word (that) he did not know how much he had on board.

About noon he sent a few things with which I expected to bring up my arrears of provisions of yesterday, and issue for today tomorrow's and half of Monday's making a week and a half, but before I got through with this, both my Bread and Flour came to an end - besides that, there was no Rum at all to be issued. This kind of proceeding is certainly not to be borne.

In the morning I had a full meeting of the Officers about getting the Maroons to work to clear a plan for a Town - they agreed *Nem. Con.* After this business was settled I was applied to by the General and the rest to get them their share of the Spanish prize *in kind*.[48] I promised to apply to Sheriff on the subject.

In the evening, D. Harding arrived from Town full of a complaint he had to lay against Hobard Jarrett for disputing his authority and collaring him at the church today. I know H. Jarrett is a proud, troublesome, dog. Gave Captain Smith last night and the General today, hints about forming a Company of Maroons.

⋘ SUNDAY 19TH OCTOBER.

Took salts this morning to carry off a curious, but very troublesome kind of heartburn I've had for these 3 or 4 days.

Macaulay and Tolley called before I got out of bed. I thought it no sin to be late in bed today I assure you after fagging hard last night till 9 o'clock. Called to see Sam Sewell and saw Cyrus Williams returned [?] Wrote to Dr. Chadwick for some medicines which he sent. Had Capt. Smith to dinner with me.

⋘ MONDAY 20TH OCTOBER.

The two companies for today turned out but badly -mustered only about 16 for about 50 but Johnston reserves himself for another day. The Governor, Chadwick, Macaulay and Tolley passed the forenoon with us here, and we went on board after Dinner.

We had the unexpected company of Sheriff, Lieu. Smith, Cox and Gray who had just returned from Bana [for Banana?] Island and Hermitage joined us in Granville Town.

The Governor gave us his sanction to what I have done in regard to provisioning the Maroons, but I could not get him to prescribe for the home coming - never mind - as I cannot help it -I will continue to do my best - so whoever blames me, George Ross, will never blame himself - no don't!

The Governor took a walk with me to see intended Hospital and approved the measure. I then pointed out to him Jack Jarrett, and in the course of a short conversation that followed, I was glad to perceive that I am not likely to be bound for a Journal from Halifax [?].

Sent my Gun to Town and had it changed - thanks to Tommy Fothingill!

☙ *TUESDAY 21ST OCTOBER.*

Slept on board last night. Mustered only 25 for the companies of Gray and G. Lawrence today - only half their quotes, but they wrought [?] well - and so did Palmer's detachment.[49] *as it is said* [in very fine hand and underlined].

Began receiving the Boxes etc. of the Maroons last night from on Board. Who will be answerable for the things that are missing?[50]

Between seeing the Companies at work, making out and calling the provision List, and examining and receiving the Baggege, this was a very busy day with me.

Wrote a few lines to Sheriff in the evening about a division of the Prize Sugar and to let me have my mess Bill.

☙ *WEDNESDAY 22ND OCTOBER.*

Went out with Capt. Smith in the morning to see sick people, viz., Sewell, Mathison, and Ellis' child.

Receiving and delivering Maroons Boxes all day. Hermitage sent me a piece of fresh pork. Jarrett and Col. Johnson, out with their companies today - 39 in number.

On my return in the morning the General and Baily - who,I observe, is always first and too forward in any ploy, came to tell me a long palaver. The General's prepare war a good and a very sensible one - indeed, full of good, manly sense: and expression of Veneration and gratitude to that Being who was kind to us in preserving us from the dangers of the sea - but it was so very long that it was a good while before I could learn what he would be at. It was no less than that I would countenance and aid the Maroons in requesting the Governor to let the Rebels who were consigned to Bullom come and live with us here and enjoy their old lands, etc; that the Maroons did not wish that any people should be drove away from their places for them etc. etc. I told the General (that) his information was not so good as his motives were humane and generous; he had only come to this country as (early as) yesterday - the people who were now about to be removed to the Bullon Shore had not at this time first forfeited their right to the lands they occupied. I gave him a history of the place and the groundless dissatisfactions of Settlers etc., etc.

After all I said, tho' he by no means showed any disposition to apply to the Governor without my consent, - but on the contrary said I was his Father, and he should always be guided by me - yet, as I perceived him very intent and indeed urgent on the business, I told him I saw no harm that could come of his applying to the Governor, being well assured that if the Governor did not comply, he would give him reasons that would satisfy him he should not.

I then addressed a line to the Governor telling him that it appeared that the Bullomites he had let loose upon us had been tampering with the Maroons in consequence of which the General had a request to make of a rather curious nature.

I by no means had approved of letting those same Bullomites loose upon us and I had no objection to the Governor's seeing this much of the effect of the measure.

Baily had another suit which he was equally urgent with - it was about Sam Thorpe and his brother.

Before I set out this morning I saw Sam give his brother a most wicked threshing in the street - I made him desist. On enquiring, I found Tom had in the night got foul of a rather too yound girl, which occasioned no small uproar being detected in the night. A few minutes after this, as I was going out of Town, Baily came up to me and demanded that Tom should be had up for judgement and punishment. I told Baily I was now going out of Town, but at my return, I should hear what he had to say on two points - 1st, the punishment to be inflicted on Sam Thorpe for taking the punishment of his brother in his own hands - and then, all circumstances considered, the punishment to be inflicted on his brother. As soon as it was agreed that he and the General should go to Town, he began afresh with this business. I told him to settle one matter first.

I shall call no meeting of Maroon officers for any such purpose while I have only - as at present - verbal commission, tho' I see *order* must suffer from it.

The General returned in the evening in high spirits. He brought me a letter from the Governor and another from Smith (Secretary) - they thought it a very serious business I find on the Hill. [The Bullomites?] I could have told them they had no occasion [unfinished sentence].

The General staid the evening. I went to make some Punch to sweat away my sore throat - and the General thinks I make good Punch. We were very high, talking away upon the dash the General should cut tomorrow at his intended visit to King Tom.[51] Captain Smith and D. Shaw were present when Baily came in in haste and told us Barnet had killed Fanny Williams. We ran to Fanny Williams' hut and found her not dead but not far from it - weltering in blood and still bleeding from several deep stabs she had got in the Breast.

She was not to be saved: she died $1/4$ of an hour later. Before she died, Barnet's brother came in from the country and told us he (his brother) had gone home and shot himself.

Our attention was next taken up by one of Coup's [?] wives -daughter of Fanny Williams whom Barnet had also stabbed in the heart. I went to her Tent - there was a great deal of halloring. I put myself in mind of Lefevre* - they all cried, 'she'll die,' I said 'she will not die,' and so on.

There was knocked up such a halloring - several Maroons were unfortunately the worse of liquor. I [placed?] Captain Smith in charge to set a watch of 6 for the night and himself to command them for the preservation of order.

I then went home and wrote a line to the Governor acquainting him of the circumstances and gave it to Smith to send the first of day light (sic).

It was a most rainy night and when I went to turn in I found my bed all wet - not so good for a sore throat, neither.

Let me see what sick people etc., I supplied today: sugar to John Ellis' child, and in the evening, a candle and half a Gallon of Rum for *the death of the said child*.

Sugar for Sewell - for Cooper - for Jarrett - for Scarlett, and a great many more of them. In short, my expenditures at present are from the very nature of them incalculable tho' there were more hands than one

* See page 41 and 65.

to keep an account of them. I must still hold by the doctrine I have had occasion some time since to lay down for myself viz:

To do the best the present circumstances will admit of and leave the rest to providence. That is, I act for the S.L. Co^y and without being particularly restricted - let me then do the most I can for promoting their Interest, and if they don't reward, tis not my fault - if in the end I find myself Debtor, tis my misfortune.

∾ THURSDAY 23RD OCTOBER

Went to see, with the General, William Barnet, dead. Received the Governor's answer to my letter - they won't interfere.

Called a meeting of the Chiefs - the greatest harmony prevailed. Sent to Hermitage to make Coffins and to mark out the burying grounds. The woman is to be buried decently; the young, after sunset in a corner of the burying ground.

This affair made the General put off his visit to King Tom. Dr. Chadwick came up in the morning and was afraid we should lose Coup's wounded wife.

Allowed the Maroons their usual Division on (the) occasion of this woman's burying [burial?] till 8 o'clock in the evening.

Got Captain Smith and Jarrett to be joint Stewards and *conservators* of the peace during the ceremony. Jarrett has all this day behaved uncommonly well - and a fine fellow he is when he chuses to conduct himself well; he is a great Man in great matters; he acts nobly - and if he is engaged in small matters, his genius and manner is such that by foul means or fair, he makes them of consequence.

Drunken Baily - to my no small annoyance got stuttering Elliott to chant over the corpse before burial.

- 'tis true that at the desire of the Maroons I read prayers over the grave - much the better for that no doubt!^{52}

Some of the Maroon songs sung this evening were being *interpreted* — 'We are sorry for what has happened but we can't help it - let us drink and be merry - and be friends to, and support one another.'

'Pity it is to see her friends bereft of Fanny Williams.'

And last night, when the woman was al - [most]* dead and intelligence had not yet arrived that Barnet [had]* made away with himself - the old General [started singing]* a koromantyn^{53} song with great earnestness - [and this]* electrified all the Maroons who heard it - 'Blood has been shed [and]* Shaw Barnet has done the deed - he has fled - let him be pursued and taken that justice [and]* vengeance may seize him'

---

*Damaged manuscript and the editor has inserted the words in square brackets that would fit in with the sense of the text.

Yet the Old Man tonight, to my no small surprize recollected not a word of it. Had the General, Palmer, Charles Shaw etc., with me this evening - and we were very jovial. The poor General was quite down all day - had not a word to say for himself, till a Glass of Punch and Rosy [?] brought him to - and then he did speak.

Second Note Book

↩ FRIDAY 24TH OCTOBER.

Went to Town and staid all night at the Government House.

I do not dislike the probable result of our conference for he, [the Governor] on suggestion, encouraged my openly calling for my appointment being specified.

Called on Wilson - he won't be Sheriff. Mary - Bob Brown's daughter died today. Gave 1/2 gallon of Rum for her burial.

-Strange that Maroons should be sure to get drunk on the death of their nearest relatives. Witness Bob Brown, Sam Shaw and Ellis.

↩ SATURDAY 25TH OCTOBER.

The Doctor accompanied me out in the morning.

Wrote to the Governor and Council - issuing provisions all day and visiting and assisting the sick - and shame to tell it, abused by one whom I assisted - but he should feel - he shall smart for his most unreasonable abuse if I have anything to say with the Maroons.

Old Phibe Stone died today and I issued another 1/2 gallon of Rum to have her out of the way.

The old General poorly today - gave him a Bottle of Gin.

↩ SUNDAY 26TH OCTOBER.

Macaulay called before I got out of bed with letters from his brother, [letters from?] my father and brother and Crispi, which came last night by the *Asprey*.

I had a great many visits to make to the sick before I got to Town - I had a snack with Hermitage.

Saw Smith,[54] who is come out in the *Asprey* - he seems of a very *familiar cast* - but paws off Pompey!

The Governor told me that as (of) now the Charter of Justice has come out and people should be appointed who should have suffi-

cient power to ratify Maroon marriage concerns.[55] He could not think
of sacrificing three days to the job - 'just as you will.'

The General and his suite paid a visit to King Tom today.

Wilson came out with me in the afternoon.

☙ MONDAY 27TH OCTOBER.

Colonel Johnson went to town with James Laurice and Rushin to
speak about a compensation for things taken Out of their Boxes on
board the *Asia.*

I sent a line to the Doctor telling him that the number of our Sick
was fast increasing. He came out in the evening with Macaulay but
went on board with him almost immediately again; was sent out in the
afternoon and visited the sick.

☙ TUESDAY 28TH OCTOBER.

The Doctor went round the sick and pronounced only 3 sick cases.

I had a letter from the Governor in the afternoon informing me of
the circumstances, took no further notice of it in my answer than
telling him that whatever sick cases there were when Chadwick set
out from here, there were three fresh ones waiting my return from
convoying him. In the Governor's letter he mentioned that Bright
would write to me soon, if he had not done it already on the subject
of my last note.

Old Palmer gave up the Ghost this afternoon, as did a daughter of
Tom Harding. Palmer's burial cost us 6 Bottles of Rum - I went in the
evening to see their frolic - how they did it up to be sure!

Harding's daughter, being *but of yesterday* was put off with half a
Gallon.

☙ WEDNESDAY 29TH OCTOBER.

So it seems that tho' there were but three sick cases yesterday at
Noon - before Noon today we have had as many deaths -for this
morning a child of Sam Stone's gave up breathing.

What a blow up! What a rugged piece of business this morning
between Palmer and Jarrett - about young Tom Palmer's affair with
young Miss Jarrett - but we got over it!

Busy day in serving out provisions for a week - all except Rice,
which we have not - for that which we had, upon opening the Cast,

proved of no use - bad - heated - good for nothing.

∾ THURSDAY 30TH OCTOBER.

Went to Town in the morning intending to see the Governor, but the first I saw of him was at his receiving on shore the Captain of the *Asprey* and his Lady. I therefore did not chuse making myself an unseasonable visitor, but having Captain Smith with me, I walked up to the mountain, that is, to Rose Hall and came home by Washington's.

∾ FRIDAY 31ST OCTOBER.

Went to Town again and saw the Governor and had a long chat with him - hang it! I have been deceived. The Inquisition (is) right here still. I don't like it. - so there *begins the first* of what will by and by, no doubt, be termed my *disaffection*. I am not disaffected to the interest of the Sierra Leone Company - but I never will mortify my honest nature by giving countenance to any Inquisitional system, or anything that resembles it. If I am, on Monday next, to be sworn in for an Alderman, where's harm if I had before today been made acquainted with the circumstances - Men are not Foot-balls. I don't know whether prudence and sound policy would not have dictated an enquiry into how far such an office is compatible with that to which they are thinking of appointing me - but they shall have their own way - at least until it seems in opposition with mine -and as Jarrett says - 'then is my time to peaky.'

I dined with Wilson who afterwards gave me a Sail in his Boat.

∾ SATURDAY 1ST NOVEMBER.

Had a note from Pickering today telling me to inform the Maroon officers that the Governor and Council wanted their attendance on Monday morning on Thornton to *help* to receive this same Charter from His Majesty.

In the evening Wilson brought me up Bright in his Boat. They, with Hermitage, waited till half past 9; but, on Major Baily's coming in and telling us that he expected young Jarrett would, before morning, visit Captain Smith to *kill him*, they soon sheered off.

After they were gone, I called on Jarrett. He promised to go to bed and lie still till morning and then I promised to hear what he had to say.

I turned Smith out of his bed, and got him to come to sleep in my house for the night.

✑ *SUNDAY 2ND NOVEMBER.*

Before daylight, word was brought to Rozy that her sister had fainted away - and yet before it was light we got account of her death.

- Unfortunate Baily - will nothing teach you sobriety? I have been punishing you for a week - yet though you see your daughter at death's own door, you won't lay it to heart - you confessed last night that you were the worse for liquor and therefore could not conceal what you know of Jarrett's intentions - and now - this morning you are violently drunk and outrageous. You will have drumming over your daughter, tho' I don't consent to it! Then at least let me, by the favour of you not to strike up before I shall have left town, for I am presently going to set out for Freetown. [then, at least, do me the favour not to strike up before I shall have left Town, for I am presently going to set out for Freetown: a free translation.]

I went to Freetown and laid both Jarrett's and Baily's affairs before the Governor. He promised to write me on the subject tomorrow morning, and I (am) determined in my own mind, that if I did not receive this letter before 12 tomorrow, I should give in my resignation by the same day. What a Tornado I had in the Bybrook, going home.

✑ *MONDAY 3RD NOVEMBER.*

I had a letter from the Governor before 8 o'clock desiring I should proceed according to the Maroon custom in trying Jarrett. I answered it immediately, stating how this offense would have been tried in Nova Scotia and pointing out the deficiencies which at present existed between the forms in both parts[?].

I also gave him an account of the proceeding(s) yesterday among the Maroons offer I had left them - how some, from what I had said, had turned advocates against the Drum, and carried the day -and among them, much to his praise, was young Barney Baily. I, by and by, received this answer of the Governor and Council appointing me to nominate what persons I thought proper to try the offenders and preside on the occasion myself - also expressing their high sense of Barney Baily's meritorious conduct.

I called several Maroon officers and had young Jarrett tried. -

Whoever likes a good long story loses by my being *Myself* on this occasion, and being in haste to add to the bargain, or this trial might have been made to tell well! [Regrettably lost to history]

☙ TUESDAY 4TH NOVEMBER.

Received this morning from the Governor and Council the appointment of Superintendent of the Maroon Settlement. The letter which conveyed it, which, no doubt flowed from the pen of Bright, was very handsome indeed, and expressive of the most liberal Sentiments on the part of the Gov, and Council. (See letter II, Appendix I.) Its my misfortune that I can return no compliment in kind - but hang it! Let deeds approve the Man - and I shall be at least as little behind hand as I can. I also received from the Governor a plan of Granville Town and hints upon the laying of it out.

Chadwick and Hermitage came up in the morning and stayed all day.

I certainly was feasted in the afternoon with first Lieutenant Smith's account of his most complete triumph over Sheriff and the same repeated and enlarged upon, by Chadwick who was present at the time.

Had a few of the officers with me in the evening talking over the distribution of the Town Lots in order to fix upon the best plan - gave them a dinner.

☙ WEDNESDAY 5TH NOVEMBER.

Had Lieu. Smith and Macaulay to Breakfast with me today.

Chatted over the distribution of the Town Lots with a committee of the Maroon officers and settled the manner of it. Received a letter from the Governor saying that tomorrow is appointed to receive the Charter - and, which I took as handsome of him, he sent a printed Notice of it, and a Boy and Drum, but gave the Boy no order to publish.

Had a meeting of Maroon officers and determined that the Town Lots should be drawn for.

Took a walk in the country in the afternoon to look out [?] all the bachelors - what a dismal deal of sickness there is amongst them!

Received from the *Asia*, 4 carts flour, 4 Dollars Beef, and 2 Dollars Pork and [?] of wine.

Had a letter from Smith (Alexander - Governor's Secretary) telling me that Dr. Bird[56] was to come.

✑ THURSDAY 6TH NOVEMBER.

Bird came last night. I went to Town today with the Maroon officers - we started from Government House to receive the Charter at 9 o'clock. It was well delivered and received.

We then proceeded to the church with it where the Governor opened it and it was read by Alex Smith from the Pulpit. The appointments of the Governor and Council were read and they were severally sworn in, as were the Mayor, two Aldermen, and Sheriff. The business went on well and there was a good deal of saluting from the Town and the four Vessels in the Harbour.

There was a large Dinner at Government House in the evening and after it Bumpers went round for Toasts - that's a bad fashion. It was too late before I secured a retreat as I found to my woeful experience when I tumbled off the Trees in the big Brook on my way home at 10 o'clock - indeed, shame altho' it be, it was as much as I *could do* to take myself home. I am pretty well today, the huraah - thank God - except (for) a few wounds - that is, *bruises*, but what must be the case of the others, for I left them all hard at it, toasting and hurrying away.

✑ FRIDAY 7TH NOVEMBER.

I walked to the General's in the morning and own I was a little impressed with his remarks. I was relating to him the adventurers of the last night - particularly of the fall I had into the Big Brook. He remarked with an appearance of real concern that, 'Gar Almighty stood my friend - or by Gar I should have perished' - and then, said the poor old fellow, 'What would become of me'?

I had him to Breakfast with me and sent him his dinner and supper. He is a good old man. I esteem him.

I had congratulations from all the officers in the course of the day as they heard of my escape; with no small animadversions from several for attempting the path by myself in the night and expressing how ready they should all be at any time to attend me.

Hermitage came up in the afternoon and brought me the plan again, and I find there are not sufficient of lots laid out.

Bird had 84 on his sick list today. I went to Cox and got the body of a Bullock for them.

In the evening apportioning it with Bird and Smith for tomorrow morning.

∾ SATURDAY 8TH NOVEMBER.

Disposed of our Bullock in the morning. Chadwick came up by Fly and Hermitage then sent an apology on board the *Asprey*.

What a family I've got! Only Mary well now - and I cannot get Mary kept in the house.

Smith tells me the Governor and Council will accompany Captain Watts up here on Monday morning.

So Mamadoo Murphy tells me that my old friend Mamadoo Sambo is not dead yet, but has lately been very ill.

Only think of Captain Parkinson sending last night the measure of his child for a Coffin who is not dead tonight - he ought to be horse-whipped.

I received today for the Maroons - prize, amounting to [?] wet sugar and delivered it to Jarrett, Gray and Smith; - also received Rice and Rum from their store - true, I gave Captain Gray today 1/2 Gallon of Rum to drink long life to his Grandson, *dropt this morning*- son to Boyse Harding.

∾ SUNDAY 9TH NOVEMBER.

Bert Parkinson's child is dead today. On comparing circumstances - only observe that Parkinson, the most rebellious and determined to be obstinate and ungovernable, last Sunday on occasion of the cry of his niece, who died that morning, has his subordination put to the test fairly on this (the succeeding) Sunday, by the death of his own son! - but not a word of it - quiet as Lambs - a great step gained indeed.

Took a dose of Salts today. Mary down too! Wilson paid me a visit in the afternoon, and if what he tells me of a certain department in Freetown be true, - nor may I doubt Wilson's word -there is certainly more iniquity carrying on there than was ever meant to be counte-nanced by the Sierra Leone Establishment - and undoubtedly more than becomes a Mayor's court to countenance - but we shall see.[56]

∾ MONDAY 10TH NOVEMBER.

The Governor and Council - Smith, Sheriff and Edgworth did visit us today - but Watts was unwell and unable.

Wilson was good enough to send me a kid with which, and some salt meat, I was enabled to satisfy their cravings - poor Bright took ill.

We had several little palavers - or *Confabs*- if you please, trying as much as possible to set Sheriff's deranged matters on some fair basis to proceed upon.

Of our present Governor and Council, one good thing is, that if one is young and the other easy, they both really seem to desire what is right.

Oh mon[r] [monstrous?] Fever - my old Friend, how have you been this long time. You're kind in the extreme - first to upset all my Family and then lay sieze to myself - well, here's at you [apparently taking a drink of medicine.] - Now for a hearty sweat and some Laudanum.

∾ TUESDAY 11TH NOVEMBER.

Last night I sweated 4 shirts and all my bed-clothes most completely - but I sweated still more than that for I sweated out the fever - and I can assure you I had a very decent allowance of him (the fever) last night. Took Bark this morning and plenty all day, and was, besides, from breakfast time till night, in the store, - being delivering day, and having nobody to assist me.

Doctors! - gave in a sick list, to have their Rum stopped, and upon their going to him one by one, he constantly recanted. As old Montague says, when he wants to lower one, 'Who are you? You're Nobody' - And so is our doctor from this specimen.

[unintelligible] Lawrence's wife died today. George, her son, being well in my opinion, and pledging himself for any noise that should ensue, I gave him in advance 3 gallons of rum - more particularly, as we cannot have a coffin in time to have her out of the way tonight - and the Maroons have no idea of letting their dead enjoy the *sweets of solitude*, until they are underground.

Received from the Store 1½ tons rice and 4 cwts. yams as the storekeeper and Master Edmunds are pleased today.

∾ WEDNESDAY 12TH NOVEMBER.

Too much Fever last night again - and so destitute of attendance, by the sickness of all about me as well as Rozy's attendance at her aunt's wake, (so) that I could get nothing warm, far less - anything from the Doctor. Better mind the living than the dead Rozy - they are at least most likely to thank you.

Sick enough and had to keep the house all this day taking Bark but eating nothing. Poor David Shaw dead; sent the major, on this occasion, 6 gallons of rum.

✍ THURSDAY 13TH NOVEMBER.

We had very fortunately a tornado this afternoon, and it brought me an appetite - salt pork and cold rice are pleasant dishes when I'm hungry - tho' but newly out of the fever.

D. Shaw was buried this afternoon with military honours - Home - blown[?] guns fired.

✍ FRIDAY 14TH NOVEMBER.

Had to leave my Bed and House in the night - Smith's wife, who was my lodger, being brought to Bed. Slept the remainder of the night in the store.

In the morning took a walk down towards the store - why could we not see Thornton Hill from the superintendent's house, by cutting away a few trees. Let us climb a tree here and see.

What a nice thing it will be to have a telegraph between Thornton Hill and this place.

Chadwick and Pickering came here this morning. So Pickering has burnt the Books.[?]

✍ SATURDAY 15TH NOVEMBER.

Had to be much in the hot, hot, sun all this day, seeing about the allotment of this town. It has really been a day of much fatigue to me - got the Lots drawn, but the Maroons, hang them, did not pay that punctual attention - which they ought to -particularly Colonel Johnson, who, I am sorry to say it, I have not caught sober these several days - but I must give him a rubbing up.

Charles Shaw has been as fortunate in the lots he drew as poor Smith was unfortunate.

I was very mad with the General today, and but for his illness would have given him a most severe reprimand. Upon Sam Shaw's story he forsooth sent for me to see why I was taking his lot from Harris (an old settler) hey! hey! what! then I am to be asked why I do wrong, and told to do right by you! - General! but for your weakness I am more disposed than ever I was to be very angry with you. However, let me tell you that if you give an ear to such Fellows as this is, you will fall very much in my esteem - oh, I was quite mad.

A little child of John Ellis' died today. I ordered 1/2 a gallon of rum for its (sic) grave. Sent for 20 lbs. more sugar for the sick. I'm afraid we shall have a long bill for sugar and candles - but it seems impossible to help it while the doctor tells me he has 132 upon his list.

I believe it was today I lent Captain Smith (and his wife Mary) $12 [D'12]

♥ *SUNDAY 16TH NOVEMBER.*

Macaulay came in the morning and brought 3 barrels flour and 3 Tierces Beef - fine Sunday work. Took a passage in his boat down and went to church and dined with Hermitage and sailed up with Wilson and Carr and blowed up Colonel Johnson [?] and after two or three ends [Errands?] more went to bed - any why mightn't I do so now? - pleasant dreams!

♥ *MONDAY 17TH NOVEMBER.*

Another fatiguing day - pointing out their Lots to the Maroons.

Hobart Jarrett: Old Hobart returned his Ticket for Lot 20 today - it was drawn for him by Morgan, but he says he is sick and wants none. I own I feel pleased at this, in proportion as I felt annoyed at the prospect of this old Rebel coming in my neighbourhood - no Lot drawn gave me so much annoyance as this -now I'm satisfied. I only now want to have that old stupid grumbling dog Davy Bonard a few hundred yards further off - and then I think I'd do. Oh! its a sweet thing to have a pleasant neighbourhood! witness mine at present, when I'm waked and kept awake almost every night with drunken family squabbles.

A son of Sam James' died today and I gave half a gallon of rum.

♥ *TUESDAY 18TH NOVEMBER.*

Delivery day - and a very troublesome one, having lost our sheet anchor [?] by Smith's being laid up. And poor Charlie Shaw too, who took his Berth [?] had fever on him all day - and yet thee grumblingly dissatisfied dogs would have us go again to serve them, who did not think proper to *find* it convenient to attend while the store was open.

What a bother to be sure, to have Hermitage and Chadwick quartered on me when I have nobody so much as to dress me a bit of salt meat.

Witness my having to brush a pair of shoes for myself this morning; the second pair I have had brushed these ten days - Ah well!

The Old General too bothering us with all the old woman's tales his frightful, feverish brain gathers from Sam Shaw and his dawdling son, Mason - hang the fellow - let him either die or get well and then we'll know what to do with him.

Had to check Elliott and Stoddard tonight - and I have a Decay [?] upon my lungs too - *so says Bird.*

℘ WEDNESDAY 19TH NOVEMBER.

N.B. was unwell through the night from having, in the hurry of yesterday, gulped my Dinner in place of eating it.

Went to Freetown early in the morning and passed the day there - breakfasted with Hermitage, lunched at Government House and dined with Cox.

Rebels Anderson, Stober and Waring brought in today by the Natives.

Had a long chat with the Governor on many subjects relating to the Maroons, but could hit on no plan of accomodation for Fothingill here - tho' here he must come - thats pozz [that's positive?]

Had a very troublesome visit of Prince Tom, against [after?] my arrival from Freetown this evening.

Paid Macmillan's Bills today in full. Learnt that Smith never called at my Brother's while in Edinburgh - not good (on) his part I'm sure.

[An entry of about 10 lines not intelligible]

℘ THURSDAY 20TH NOVEMBER.

Morgan's daughter died this morning, which cost half a gallon.

Visiting the sick - say [saw?] Gray, Shaw, Bernard today; pointing out Lots and accompanying Hermitage in determining the Company's Boundary Line.

-poor Smith, very low today - had him removed in the evening from the Store tomy House.

Engaged Tom Reid as Messenger at £36 currency per annum, to commence from tomorrow.

What's the reason I have always found those pretty King's Fishers [?]-harder to shoot than any other Bird.

It is a wonder with what seeming reluctance those same Maroons talk of going to the mountains to live-how can we account for this? If not from the natural sociability of the animal-man.

So I hear Cooper was sworn in yesterday for pin' [?] Alderman - good luck to him!

✍ *FIRDAY 21ST NOVEMBER.*

Morgan's daughter died this morning - poor man [unintelligible] All this day, doing all that man could do, I believe, to please the people, in the appointment of their Town Lots - by swapping and so forth. Time only can tell whether I should be able to succeed *tolerably*- more, I don't expect. At present, I own, I have to endure some rough rubs. [A few lines here not intelligible.]

All the world, collected for the purpose, would not be able to lay out the lots of this Town to the satisfaction of all the Maroons. So far as one man could have succeeded in the business, I think I have hitherto - then why should I complain?

Unsupported as I have hitherto stood, it is perhaps astonishing how well I come on. Were I supported - what a nice body of mess they would very shortly appear; for instance, show me one good subject of all the Maroons who is not pleased and satisfied - no, I'll defy you, and I'm glad to say it, the number - the proportion of bad men is but small.

Gave Captain Parkinson a gallon of rum for having built the first house on his own lot.

Hermitage brought out the theodolite today and Reid is to show us the marked tree. Reid did, doubtless, shew us the tree which had been marked by Macaulay and Domingo. I suspect however, it leaves out the Bay and Pullan [?] Tree, but it takes in a nice sweep of the mountain, and, I am sure, many a good coffee tree. From the information I have now on the subject, and (from) my own observations, I am disposed to think that Macaulay, in marking this tree for the boundary, made the Company at least 4 chains to the Westward of the first treaty and intention.

Oh! Tom, King Tom was here this morning paying his respects to Montague.

✍ *SATURDAY 22ND NOVEMBER.*

Hermitage looking out for a berth for a wharf this morning. Macaulay, Smith and Chadwick came up in the morning. I told Chadwick pretty plainly that he must know better on future what is going on in his own Department - that Bird must apply to him for the necessary supplies for the sick.

Shabby scoundrel Sheriff must be to put those poor Maroons off still, by telling them I am to receive their rum for them.

Captain Smith's youngest son, who was born under this roof but the other morning is *gone-dead;* the little stranger seems to have but called for his half gallon out of us. He saw we had too much trouble around us - 'tis a smoky house,'* squeaked the little thing - 'the sooner I'm out of it, the better,' and took his departure. But might not he have done better? for those who work out the day are likely to sleep sounder when the night comes. Well! So may it be with us, poor vagabonds.

A child of old Tom Bucknor died this evening - sent a gallon to David Bucknor.

From 1 o'clock till dark I walked about the houses of the Maroons in the country and many are the scenes of misery and sickness I witnessed. [Apparently Chadwick is being blamed here in a sentence not intelligible.]

A man that can make a mere sham of showing himself here two days in the week to increase his salary, but takes no other trouble than telling the General he has spoken to the Governor to send him wind and succeeded!

But now, I have down what in my power lay to alleviate distress through this day. Let me now - why should I put this on one side [unintelligible]

Scramble this far if you're able, and give me some Brandy and water - Now for the little vagabonds once more - Sweethearts and Wives [most certainly under the influence of the Brandy - the very writing has manifestly changed and is hardly intelligible.]

☙ SUNDAY 23RD NOVEMBER.

Walked into Freetown in the morning and God knows, to whatever account it may go in the Books above, that my business was more to make some suitable provision for the necessities of the Maroons than to show myself in Church - to hear, as Macaulay says, King's English clipt, but to Church I did first go.

- Church - Church! Why, I mean merely the *House* which, on weekdays is occupied by MacMillan and a parcel of children, they call scholars, and, of a Sunday, where people generally meet to praise God. But they know best who made the Prayer. What was meant by the same word Church - after praying for the Governor and Council - Colony, Magistrates, etc. etc., these and all other Blessings for them,

---

*The reference to Lefevre on p.27 and now to a "smoky house," repeated on p.65, is definitely from Lawrence Sterne's, *Life and Opinion of Tristan Shandy*, a novel that clearly has some effect on Ross's prose style.

for us, and the *whole Church* - whole Botheration! But I beg their pardon - they will, I daresay, here bless Men. However, as it happens that I am not blessed with an understanding similar to theirs, I can see no cause why I should use their phrases. In them it might be proper and pious - God knows all things - but I cannot repeat the phrase - even in my heart, without a sneer at the whole bunch of canting pretenders to religion - and particularly the rotten cluster of Bishops, Deacons, and all the rest that keep eternally sounding those indefinite words in our ears and would fain have us believe that if we don't stickfast to some cluster or other which they choose to style *Church*, we shall, when we come to the other side of the water, be looked upon as a parcel of odd straggling vagabonds, and be - in short be damned. I hear them, liberal Souls!

-Oh poor little things. They have been bred to think as they tell us, and I don't blame them. But I must blame myself, and that most severly (for I) did once harbour the thought that the God who judges of us according to our actions, is not as good a judge of a good heart and a good action in our part of the world, and in our situation in life as another - 'in our part of the world' - I mean nothing more than the difference between being outside of a Church or out of a Church - or of no Church - and being in, or of, or belonging to a Church sect.

-What a Dance this same Church has let me! But now, should any one who knows the manner in which I have been brought up, fancy that sentiments like the above proceed from a rooted dislike of the manner of my upbringing - or to religion generally, I must undeceive them. The spring from which it all proceeds - and I believe it has always been the strongest spring about my heart, is; the detestation in which I hold everything that tends to *enslave the Mind* - 'tis a hard, hard, thing to have a man's body in duress - but his Mind - oh heavens! Let it have its way and short of heaven it won't stop. [Ross, in his own way, is a typical product of the Scottish Enlightenment with its rugged individualism and its savage love of liberty].

Hey - hey! where have I got to? Not quite so fast - Sierra Leone to wit.

Talking with Hermitage today, about the probable time the Superintendent's house would be finished, he told me I need not expect it in 3 months.

Coming home, I formed a resolution of knocking up a bit of Hut for myself in the meantime. And I will do it too - So help(sic).

I told Hermitage that however I put up with the very great inconvenience he himself was witness to, I notwithstanding thought it by no means handsome of the Governor to tell him he need not be in a hurry about my house. Nor was it handsome - nor was it fair -neither should I have expected it of Mr. Ludlam. However, when things come crops upon us so, we must rough them out.

ᴇᴏ *MONDAY 24TH NOVEMBER.*

A child of old Hutchins Stone dying [died?] this morning -cost us half a gallon.

Smith had a curious turn in his sickness last night. Nothing here but sickness! dear, dear, dear, when will there be an end? I think I must commence surgery or apothecary or something. The poor creatures generally show a great deal of confidence in me - and, which I am not glad to see, their care about Bird seems to be very little. But I don't think its altogether without a cause - for I found him out today in one most palpable lie about a vomit[?] he said he had given to old Barnet. Besides, his eating so much, and drinking so much does not show quite so well.

Gave Rushin a letter I wrote on Saturday to Sheriff about Maroons' rum. Rushin brought us up a Bullock for which I paid him 2 shillings.

Blowed Palmer up for beginning building his house yesterday on his next neighbour's Lot.

Received some beef, pork, and flour from the *Asia*. Walked round by Daniel Bonard's, Parkinson's and C. Shaw's in the afternoon and was busy all day showing and appropriating Lots and visiting the sick of all descriptions - women with child[ren], [pregnant women] etc. etc. I must commence midwife[ry] by and by.

ᴇᴏ *TUESDAY 25TH NOVEMBER.*

Delivery day. Fothingill came up to look on - he sneers most apishly at everything he sees in regards to my accomodation. But I choose to undergo the hardships.

Served today only half a week's allowance which clears the Maroons to the 28th inst.

The Bullock I had slain for them was not so kindly and thankfully received as I had reason to expect. Those vagabonds prefer getting a few pence for their salt meat to seeing their friends recover. Only think of Colonel Johnson returning two or three pounds of fresh beef I sent him all the way from his house. That vagabond Zuaco! But I stopped his allowance for it.

♋ WEDNESDAY 26TH NOVEMBER.

Walked into town in the morning but the Governor was (had) not returned from the mountains. I learnt from Cox that he is going to charge the Maroons 80 dollars a ton for rice, tho' he owns he sells it to all the others for 64 dollars. We shan't have any more of it.

Wilson will supply us with better rice for 60 dollars. Martin Cox you may get 80 dollars for your rotten rice when you can.

Came up in the boat with Hermitage and shot two or three cranes.

Goodwin Barrett has got a son this morning and Johnson has sent today to beg for half a pound of fresh meat - how inconsistent!

John Ellis - be it remembered - because I would not interfere to make the doctor give him a piece of candle to see his sick child, said he would complain to the Governor - *mark that!*

♋ THURSDAY 27TH NOVEMBER.

Walked into town this morning again and chatted with the governor about several things.

After breakfast, the fever came pouring in upon me - hot and dry - what shall I do? Hermitage is gone with the barge and I shan't be able to walk as far as Granville Town - here comes Fothingill!

I went into Fothingill's and took a stout pint of strong Gin and water - but not a bit of sweat and I am hardly able to rise from the chair. After waiting more than one hour, I went on board the *Asia* with Macaulay - after a little pease soup and a glass of wine, I began to perspire and feel easy. I came up in the *Asia's* Boat in the afternoon.

I might have had an accident on the wharf today: Smith, fingering my gun on board, put the lock on when the hammer was down. On coming on shore, not observing this, I loaded the Gun -but after it was loaded, I found to my surprise, the cock would never (move) neither one way or t'other - and the stop too, was stationary. I took up Tom Richard's hammer and went a knocking at the stop and the gun went off - providentially I held the gun at the time, in my left hand - the muzzle pointed right up.

What a piece of trouble Captain Smith has had with that same Maroon Sugar! Oh Sheriff thou art a poor creature - Worse than that - much worse - a most despicable reptile - mean abject wretch.

ᐯ FRIDAY 28TH NOVEMBER.

Took some calomel pills last night which has a good effect. Bird tells me I had 12 G^{ns}. cal. and 14 G^{ns}. [?] in my dose.

I was very well in this fore part of the day and worked and walked about in the sun a great deal - and took a little dinner with a keen appetite; but alas, it checked my sweating and for the remainder of the afternoon and evening, I was in a most doleful high fever. It belongs not to this day to say when it went off.

Fothingill attended at the weekly delivering today in his own [not intelligible]

Tom Campbell's wife died this morning immediately after eating a good healthy breakfast - and as is said too, within one week of her being brought to bed.

It is supposed to be owing to a thrashing her husband is known to have given her about 3 nights ago. But bird could perceive no mark of violence on the corpse.

Oh true, nothing less than a gallon of rum went down on this occasion.

ᐯ SATURDAY 29TH NOVEMBER.

Nine sailors came here this morning in an open boat from the Rio Pongas - late belonging to the *Mercury*, Captain John Sellars. At their request, I sent for Mr. Macaulay and he came up - but before he came, the fellows got (most of them) drunk and did not know exactly what to do; but they were very noisy - at times they were for accompanying Macaulay - but then they did not altogether like it, and some of them objected strongly to the delivering up of the boat and arms they had got which belonged to the *Mercury*. I found Macaulay went away at last without them.

There was a pretty dust kicked up in the afternoon by some of our old settlers who had got drunk and fell a picking quarrels with the natives and fighting them, forsooth.

Bond and Stoddard appearing determined to renew the fight after every endeavour to pacify them - and stripping and challenging and squaring at the natives. I sent a party of Maroons with them to the Governor - Macaulay becoming bound that the natives, who were the lads belonging to the boat, should be there to answer for themselves.

When the Maroons returned, they told me that having waited 2 hours at the Governor's house, and Macaulay not making his appearance, the vagabonds were discharged - indeed, it must have been so, for Macaulay stayed lounging about here too long after they were gone.

I was tolerably well - that is, was this morning, but at 10 or 11 o'clock, how the fever did set in again!

Half a teaspoon of boiled papaw which, with a good deal of ado, I swallowed - and a wine glass full or wine and water, which I tried as an experiment, brought out a sweat and gave me ease till those vagabonds with their fighting made me turn out.

☙ *Sunday 30th November.*

Pretty wellish today - thank God! Bark away. The Master of the *Asprey* came up today with a letter from Captain Watts enclosing the Governor's letter to him. Curphy's business was to apprehend the sailors from the Rio Pongas; they had gone away last night 2 by water, 6 by land, and one, poor dog, who was not able to keep up from fever, remained behind.

Before Curphy set out, 5 had arrived in town who were immediately laid hold of, and Sheriff, with a party of the *Asprey's* people appeared - having come by land in pursuit of them from town. They dragged them all away.

What a strange Fish Watts appears to be after all! For Ludlam's marking the work *responsible* in a letter with a stroke under it, he wrote him in answer that he had not been long enough in Africa to understand the meaning of scratches under words. His letter to me is evidently written in a hurry but it carries no marks of a sound intellect.

☙ *Monday 1st December.*

Major Baily's daughter, Venus died today. Coup Smith caught a large animal of the deer kind in his trap today. Weakly today and a little feverish.

☙ *Tuesday 2nd December.*

Sent Reid to town this morning. Had Hermitage with me today and he bestowed high praises on Coup's Venison.

☙ *Wednesday 3rd December.*

Another child of old Stone's died today - ½ gallon.
Sent Tom Reid around to all the Maroons to tell them to give in

their accounts against the *Asia* by next Friday at farthest - also to make it known that firing guns on Sunday and at nights was against orders except in cases of necessity.

Corankapone and Kizell[58] were here today to see us.

Received a letter from the Governor and Council to draw up a report[59] of the Maroons since their landing, to go by the Asia, which will be ready to sail the 20th inst.

☙ THURSDAY 4TH DECEMBER.

Wrote to Chadwick today to furnish his report and bring it up to the 14th inst. as the *Asia* sails not to [until?] the 20th.

A rainy day kept me in the home a good deal tho' very little unwell.

Fothingill tells me the Governor does not go home in the *Asia*.

☙ FRIDAY 5TH DECEMBER.

So I must go without wine because I won't give Cox 80 dollars, which, with taxes and impositions coming through his hands, I may safely call 90 dollars a ton for his rice - when I get better from Wilson for 60 dollars. I may drink water but I shall discharge my duty faithfully. But what a scurvy heart must be his who stoops to show such a miserable revenge - revenge! For what? For doing my duty - but the misfortune is that my duty happens to clash with his Knavish practices. God be thanked I have got over the fever. Grog will do for me. - but I own - the Sierra Leone Company are [is?] much to blame to put it in the power of such a pitiful wretch to lock up their stores from their servants.

The Governor and Smith and Chadwick here today. The Governor, had, I believe, been entertaining thoughts of letting the Maroons have nails,etc., and yet he disclaims having Smith as an accessory. I should not like to catch Smith at it, I own.

Fothingill's assurance! to bring up rice from the store without consulting me. This Tommy Cox again - but, let us alone, we shall settle them, quietly too.

Right must and will prevail [unintelligible]

Peggy Gray died today. Alas old Peggy! Only half a gallon.

☙ SATURDAY 6TH DECEMBER.

Today I was able to walk about - but after a little exertion in the morning, I found if I did it, it was at the risk of a relapse. So I did greatly command myself for the greatest part of the heat of the day to stay in the house. But a piece of salt beef, tho' I have the luxury of a yam to it is no great treat to a man just getting out of his fever - but I must take the world as I find it. Could I have fresh meat, I should not have taken salt.

Engaged John Harding today to assist the surgeon at a salary of £3 per month. Paid crew men last night 6/- for carrying 1½ tons rice up from the wharf.

Bird tells me he has 155 [sick] on his list. I find there have been 22 deaths since their landing besides the old woman on board the *Asia* in the Harbour.

∾ SUNDAY 7TH DECEMBER.

Nanny - Major Baily's daughter died this morning.

I walked to town pretty early and knocked up Wilson and Hermitage. Breakfasted and dined with Wilson. I felt much refreshed - and, I don't hesitate to say - [much] benefit to my health from the jaunt. Why, indeed, it must be so. If I only remember to take the walk - for a little conversation unbends the mind, and the sight of a friend's face is not bad help — and I shall, by and by, I suppose, be saying, *A Glass of Wine* -these are such comfortable things!

I have my doubts tho' whether a repetition of the jaunt tomorrow will be advisable - tho' I should like very much to dine at Wilson's and see this business [?] made up.

Wilson talks of a trip to the Banana and Plantain Islands. I should like it very much, and it would doubtless conduce to my health but I much fear I cannot be spared. Can I?

Canting Elliot came in bothering me after my return and made me read a sermon to him - all palaver.

∾ MONDAY 8TH DECEMBER.

Walked into town to dine with Wilson. That Sheriff being of the party made me feel uneasy. What a thing it is to be in the company of a man who has no honesty.

Captain Watts and lady were here, but the Governor went up with a party to keep his harvest home in the mountain.

I returned about dark and felt amazingly fatigued - could sleep now all night.

◌ *TUESDAY 9TH DECEMBER.*

The lady I had at work on my house, told me they would strike if I did not give them 2/6 per day instead of 2/-. I shall give you no more than 2/-. If you can better yourself you are in the right to go to it.

Had a note from the Governor to dine and chat over the charter. I am not able. I must be excused. Here's a pretty joke! They think, forsooth, that I can march down in the heat of the day and back again at night; not so cheap as that neither. There is no Inn in Freetown - the least that might be made me is the offer of a bed on such occasions. Till that is the case, they may depend on it that they will find me scarce in Freetown.

Appointed today to meet the Maroons on the subject of allotting the mountain lands but hang them again, they did not attend. Tomorrow morning if they don't attend I shan't ask their advice.

Polly Chambers this morning delivered of a daughter.

◌ *WEDNESDAY 10TH DECEMBER.*

Slept remarkably well last night - tho' woke once by a rattler of a tornado - the thunder very near.

Fever returned again in the afternoon.

That Yago Barnet is certainly the most confounded and barefaced Liar that ever broke bread, except, perhaps, his namesake, Othello's counsellor. I found tonight he had got a-fetching posts to Robert Singer's Lot - half a mile, almost, from his own. Nor did he rest there but told me there was a staff driven there by him at my desire, as a mark. In coming down from showing Barnet his Lot, 'tis true that I shot a bird from Singers lot upon the adjoining one, and I believe while I was reloading, I might have informed him and his brother of the mistake Arthur Harding committed in clearing Singer's Lot in place of his own -but the very circumstance of my having known the mistake about this Lot is a most convincing proof that I never could have dreampt, I might have - but certainly not thought of giving it to him - unless I am sometimes mad.

Morgan has settled himself upon Lot 129 instead of 127, drawn by John Thompson.

Spoken to Rozy about her living in this house and her intention of continuing with me - She says yes - but we did not settle all the preliminaries.

So my good friends Chambers and the rest who were at work with me yesterday are gone off because I won't give them half a dollar for 2/-per day. I'm glad to find Hermitage of the same mind.

ᴄᴏ *THURSDAY 11TH DECEMBER.*

Alas! for my poor journal. Tis now, in fact, the 22nd of December when I write this. But if my journal suffers, it is because my poor body has suffered more. In short, on 11th, 12th, 13th and 14th, I was extremely unwell and resolved on a jaunt to Freetown to get out of this noisy neighbourhood. I wrote to the Governor and Council and they sent the Barge for me in the afternoon of the 15th.

From that time till last night I was at Wilson's recovering by degrees. God knows how I'll do now but I don't think I'll weather out long here.

ᴄᴏ *SATURDAY 20TH DECEMBER.*

Poor Ian Osborne slept off.

ᴄᴏ *SUNDAY 21ST DECEMBER.*

The choice of *Liberpool [?] came in for Boetifeur.*[60]

ᴄᴏ *MONDAY 22ND DECEMBER.*

Sessions began today. Anderson and [?][61] Guilty. Death.

ᴄᴏ *TUESDAY 23RD DECEMBER.*

The John of Liberpool came in last night. She is the store ship spoken of. I find she has boats, etc., for the Governor.

ᴄᴏ *WEDNESDAY 24TH DECEMBER.*

I was tolerably well today and felt some little appetite for my dinner; but, not an hour after, comes the fever again, pouring hot.

Spoke to Fothingill about his store arrangement but he seemed quite indifferent about the matter. Had a chat with Smith afterwards, on the same subject and laid down a plan to propose.

Ann Ellis, John Ellis' daughter died today - ½ gall.

ᴄᴏ *THURSDAY 25TH DECEMBER.*

Very unwell all day. Yago Barnet too, apprehended on his way to shoot me! A pretty Xmas box he would give me of it. Old Kitty Linton slept off today - another 1/2 gallon. Sophy, a daughter of Miss D. Heath, was last night delivered of a daughter.

✍ FRIDAY 26TH DECEMBER.

I went to Freetown in the boat I sent for last night having first settled the business of Barnet here and pardoned him upon his getting Captain Smith and Palmer to be securities for him for a 12 month.

Nothing can show in a stronger point of view, the bad effects of the absence of a police and means of inflicting punishment among us than this man's story (i.e. Barnet's) from first, all through. Through every stage of the business he was conscious of being greatly wrong and yet because at no stage of it did he receive punishment he would have proceeded to the taking of my life.

✍ SATURDAY 27TH DECEMBER.

Hot fever last night and fever and retching all day -but had to go to the doctor as he would not come to me - took an Emetic.

The Governor Ludlam offered me a part of his house till Thursday next week. I accepted.

✍ SUNDAY 28TH DECEMBER.

Took salts but they were not effectual. At night with high fever on, took two tumblers of porter with a relish of 2 purging pills.

✍ MONDAY 29TH DECEMBER.

Weakly today but better.

✍ TUESDAY 30TH DECEMBER.

Fever gone - thank God! for it kept its hold since last Friday night most completely.

✍ WEDNESDAY 31ST DECEMBER.

Had a talk with Gray but was not pleased with his putting -off system.

Wrote to the Governor and Council about my circumstances in Granville Town and that I should not return thither till they were bettered.

1801

↬ *Thursday 1st January.*

Gave in my report of the Maroons today but dated it as of yesterday's.

Dined with Hermitage. Ludlam there. Got Wilson to bring me 3 bags of sugar at 9d per lb.

A pretty strong Harmattan. Wilson's therm. 90.

↬ *Friday 2nd January.*

Received answer to my letter of the 31st to Governor and Council allowing me the use of the apartment I now occupy at Government House till my house at Granville Town be finished.

Dined at Wilson's with a snug party - Gray, Bright and Carr. How weak I am!

Another Harmattan, stronger than yesterday.

↬ *Saturday 3rd January.*

Dined with Wilson at Carr's and was hardly able to carry myself up the hill afterwards.

Wrote a letter to Chamberlain in the morning. A warmish day - not a Harmattan - hazy.

↬ *Sunday 4th January.*

Wrote a letter to my father - not very well today -hazy day.

↬ *Monday 5th January.*

Intended going to Granville Town in the morning but fortunately could not get a boat for the fever was pressing hard upon me again.

The *Stranger* came in this afternoon, one month from Torbay [?] She has brought Dawes [62] and many more.

It brought a few letters. By sitting to read them in a stream of air, I contracted a pain-back of my head.

A fair enough hazy day.

◌ *TUESDAY 6TH JANUARY.*

Poorly all day. Had the new-comers to Dinner with us; Radlam [?] is a good-natured open fellow. I wonder what made them send Lee out. McNair, the Captain, is a keen Scotchman, and if you like a blunt Scotchman too.

Hazy day - all the days now are hazy. Captain G. Lawrence's son died today.

◌ *WEDNESDAY 7TH JANUARY.*

What a fever I had last night and continues today - took a large, large quantity of Bark today at the instance of W. Dawes. Poor Archy Morrison's child died today.

A coldish hazy day; sent Chadwick a strongish note and I could not help it.

◌ *THURSDAY 8TH JANUARY.*

Captain Palmer's wife and Cuffee Bucknor died today.

The *Asia* and *Asprey* sailed about 3 o'clock. What might that Sheriff mean by not giving me my account?

Wrote and sent six letters by the Asia viz., my father, brother, Crispi, Davidson. Macaulay and Chamberlain.

Bird has been engaged today at £100 p.a. Hazy day - sea breeze.

◌ *FRIDAY 9TH JANUARY.*

I begin to be rather better again, thank God.

Hazy day, little wind - rather warm.

Walked down to Wilson's in the afternoon and got a [unintelligible].

Fired a shot from the Howitzer this afternoon from the Hills which went a great way out in the River.

Jarrett and Johnson called this evening. Wrote to the Governor and Council about Maroon police.

◌ *SATURDAY 10TH JANUARY.*

Smith called this morning from Granville Town. I went with him to Wilson's and set them upon business.

Hazy - but a stout sea breeze.

So Pickering has left Thornton Hill already.

I don't know how it is but the wheels of government here seem to me to move to no time at all.

I fear that his putting off the Maroon business will turn awkwardly on them and then it will and most justly be called dim infatuation.

ꙮ SUNDAY 11TH JANUARY.

Whiled away the morning taking Bark. Afternoon went to church. What a confounded head that Butcher Smith carries about with him. Hazy day - sea breeze. Therm, 85:

ꙮ MONDAY 12TH JANUARY.

Had a chat with Bright on police for Maroons, etc. etc. Called on Gray afterwards about getting a boat for tomorrow for Granville Town. Called on Wilson and had a luncheon at Hermitage's.

ꙮ TUESDAY 13TH JANUARY.

Sent to M. Cox for the following articles on Maroon acct:
3 grms. best (?) Foolscap
6 grms. best Letter paper - plain and Gilt
(Which Mr. Cox with an app^ce. [appearance] of being in high dundgeon, refused to attend to.)
1 grm. large ffs. thin-cut
1 grm. large ffs. thick
3 memo Books, small for the pocket
2 pap£(?) Black ink powder
6 blk. lead pencil
1 Bottle Indian Rubber
14 lbs. Sealing Wax
A small quanty. wafer (?)
1-24 inch round ruler
1-12 inch round ruler
1 penknife
1 paper cutter
Some Green Tape
1 Marble [?] Corn & Ho. [?] paper book - largest Size. Attempted going to Granville Town but could not, for want of a boat. Wrote to the governor and council for a boat for the Maroon Service and had a knowing answer from Gray through Bright about this old Barge. What

cunning - how much of the Fox appears in Gray's character!

Had a chat with Dawes in the evening respecting his future intended Family establishment - oh, anything for a quiet life.

Hazy - sea Breeze, from 5 in the morning, all day!

☙ WEDNESDAY 14TH JANUARY.

Dawes entered upon his administration today - first job was the Maroons - several things were talked over and some determinations come to.

Radlam [?] appointed aide de camp.

Hazy - a kind of Harmattan.

☙ THURSDAY 15TH JANUARY.

Went down expecting to get the Barge but she was at Granville Town. Walked there and thought, 3 or 4 times I should have fainted on the way. Returned on the Barge again with 4 Maroons besides Tom Reid.

Did a good deal of business and fagged away lustily.

Dined at Gray's The *Nancy* coming in from the leewards -how knocked up I am in the evening.

Hot, hot day - clearest day this fortnight, but still hazy.

Wilson's thermometer at 3 o'clock was 94 degrees in the shade.

☙ FRIDAY 16TH JANUARY.

Oh - what a night I had of it till 3 a.m. - in the very extreme of pain and torment with my bowels. Could neither sit, stand, lie or walk. - I thought I must have given up the Ghost. I felt this coming on in Granville Town - a kind of sensation annoyed me as though both my sides were going to fall from me.

Offered Bond 75 dollars for his Lot yesterday; gave Bird leave today to build upon Lot No. 23 - the Lot to be his during his continuance in the Company's Service, and when he is about to go, to be paid by valuation for his improvements on it.

A piece of salt beef, yams and cheese, and that was all, upon my word, - no bread even, except a piece of Cassade [Cassava?] cake, which he kept by himself. Cursed, mean spirit of him! Here I have been fasting and fagging from 8 o'clock this morning, almost dead last night, and took in my torture some purging pills which have not oper-ated, and now at 5 o'clock, behold my dinner! Nothing positively that I can either eat or drink - for the wine is cyderish sower, and sower porter, I must not drink. Here's a pretty mess I have got into - but hang me if I don't touch him up.

℘ SATURDAY 17TH JANUARY.

Thought Pickering's letter of yesterday was meant for today to attend the Corporation, and now I find the mayor and Alderman have sent our congratulatory address to the new Governor.

Well, my name is not to it, and I am *not angry.*

Wilson tells me he paid 6 dollars for proof's [?] land, and drew a bill in my name for that and [unintelligible] a very snug little dinner with Bright. Called on Gray about the boat, Davidson of the *Nancy,* has brought up - 'he'll see about it.'

A very strong Harmattan indeed - and hazy.

℘ SUNDAY 18TH JANUARY.

Went to church in the morning. Another strong Harmattan. I find these Harmattans blow up about sunrise and die away towards his [its] setting. The air towards the morning is very cool. Thermometer sometimes quite down at 72 - true!

℘ MONDAY 19TH JANUARY.

To Granville Town in the morning - had a busy day paying prize money and pointing out Lots. Truly and verily, I have found that same job of pointing out the Lots one of the most difficult jobs I ever had to do - except *writing a long letter.* But I find that (that is, the behaviour of the Maroons over their Lots) perverse cunning. After having taken possession of the Lot to which they give their preference, they try to browbeat me out of it as though I had made a mistake in shewing them their Lots. That I find to be the case with most of them. And yet, I must patiently tell such vagabonds that I am sorry that they should have mistaken their own Lots - when I would like to be laying a good Horse whip over their backs.

A young Harmattan - hazyish.

So Dawes will run out the Maroons' Land! Well, with all my heart.

℘ TUESDAY 20TH JANUARY.

Walked up to Granville Town this morning - not quite so much to do as yesterday. Met Bob Wright coming to the Governor for a Lot, there being no Lot for him, but he returned with me and took one of the *old Gave Lots*.

A light NE breeze till 3p.m., and from that time, a rather Fresh, Westerly breeze.

Received Resolutions of the Court today.

Brought down Herbert Williams to Pickering.

Governor Dawes allowed [agreed?] to let the General have the house I was building for which the poor old General was very thankful.

✑ WEDNESDAY 21ST JANUARY.

At home all day preparing a family and *neighbourly* list of Maroons for the drawing of country land.

Ellis came in to be told about his Lot, not having been given up, but fortunately, I had it in my power to satisfy him to his heart's content.

Sam Thorpe came in about his brother, John.

Wrote to Fothingill to alter the provision list. Dawes told me about the battle about the rice now waging between Ludlam and Gray; Drunk tea at Wilson's. Stout easterly breeze all day.

✑ THURSDAY 22ND JANUARY.

Walked up again in company with Montague.

Old Jarrett thought 'by God, it was hard' that they should have to pay a shilling an acre quit rent [63] for their land. Unruly man! But I got him silenced and after having finished the business I came upon, I recommended to Montague (that) if they indeed thought there was cause for complaint, they had better (certain officers) come to the Governor and Council tomorrow morning about it.

Had oatmeal porridge at breakfast.

Came down in the Barge with the General. Dawes had a public dinner but ill-attended.

Sea breeze set in about 1 o'clock. It was most shockingly hot today, to be sure.

✑ FRIDAY 23RD JANUARY.

Major Jarrett, H.N. Jarrett, Johnson, Baily, Nash Hamilton and Parkinson headed by the General waited on the Governor this morning about the quit rents. There was a great deal of talk and a great many cases proposed to shew how trifling the demand and how easily satisfied - but still there was an answer to every argument, till at last Parkinson very bluntly said that the matter was that the Maroons were not willing to pay any quit rent. Upon which Mr. Dawes, in really a manly and very determined tone told him that 'no Maroon - nor any other person should hold a foot of land in this Settlement without they paid the quit rent.' It was an ill-timed though a most pertinent remark and also a well delivered remark that Mr. Bright made immediately after: that the Company was faithful to their engagement to the Maroons and expected a like return of good faith on their part; ill-timed, I say - because certainly what Dawes had just said, demanded a long dead pause, which would certainly have ensued, and with the best effect, but for Bright's interference, which waned [?] the point.

They went away that they would give their yes or no tomorrow.

I went to Granville Town and laid out 4 lots more.

Easterly wind made us a rough passage going up.

☙ *Saturday 24th January.*

The Governor went up to Granville Town, and having taken a pretty extensive range of it, seemed much pleased with the progress they were making in the building of their houses.

Had another long palaver about the quit rent, and the Governor, having at length put the question - telling every man who refused to pay quit rent, to give in his name, and he should not be troubled with any land. In the course of 2 hours, 14 names were given in, three of whom, however, retracted and were admitted by the Governor.

Those who have given up their lands are: Miss D. Heath, Sam Horton, Robert Wright, I. Rushin, David Bucknor, William Gale, Richard Heath, John Parkinson, Thomas Morgan, and Thomas Parkinson.

The recanters are: Sam Shaw, Hugh Barnet, and Alex Forbes - Alex Forbes ought to be flogged, N.B.

We then walked to see the Boundary Tree. Becky Johnston's mother gave us a good deal of trouble about Becky's going to marry J. Williams.

Very cold last night - a little easterly breeze today - hazy of course.

ༀ SUNDAY 25TH JANUARY.

Nothing particular but went to church twice; not much wind, but of the harmattanish kind. Most completely easterly in the morning and came round to West by the afternoon. I observe it has been so, most days of this month.

ༀ MONDAY 26TH JANUARY.

To Granville - walked there and back again. Had the Lots drawn for mountain lands.

Added the names of Wheeton and Tom Brown to those who won't have land - they'll repent of it.

Mentioned to (Captain) Smith a hint I had from Dawes some 3 or 4 days since of some Rebels having settled back of us in the mountains - poor Smith! When I was regretting how sickly we were that 'he could not attempt to go - indeed, I was afraid it would knock myself up' [to fight the Rebels?] 'You go Captain, and you think I no go too?'

Colds are very prevalent. I have for my shame very bad cough and cold.

ༀ TUESDAY 27TH JANUARY.

Stayed at home making out a list of families and land for the surveyor.

Only think of that blood-sucker Chadwick, recommending to the company to charge their servants etc., for their medicines, and 'still it is very handsome of the Company to find them in medical assistance and advice gratis' - Spirits of Guest! hearest thou this?

£200 a year from the Company will not suffice that Jew besides what he makes of chance customers, on whom he has certainly bestowed more attention than on his proper patients - but he must likewise be allowed to bring his Bills against the Company's servants, settlers and Maroons. And yet he has the assurance(?) to add that the Company will gain 200% by it: that they never will. Never will the Company gain by letting Robbers loose upon their people - there is Cox already - shameful.

Harmattanish and warm.

Conversed with the Governor in the morning on my resigning of my place in the Corporation being from my appointment at Granville Town, unable to do the duties of the office. I had no objection. But upon consulting the Charter, we found that the situation could not well be given up without appearing to persons but partially acquainted with the circumstances, unfavourable to the character of the person giving up. However, I can make a sacrifice of the risk of that when real utility requires it.

☙ WEDNESDAY 28TH JANUARY.

Walked up in the morning and came down in the Barge. Receiving the guns today.

Sam Horton severely upon his repentance and pleading hard for himself; his brother Gabe and their father, came to the Governor in the afternoon.

I don't like to hear the Governor hesitate. So far, he has acted admirable in this business, but if he slackens now, 'tis a chance but all is lost.

Brown too praying heartily to be forgiven. Had the remaining 4 Lots drawn - that is, three were drawn and the last reserved for Jarrett - No. 17.

Captain Davidson, Bright etc., dined on the Hill. So Cooper, poor fellow, is no more! Warmish day, but pleasant.

☙ THURSDAY 29TH JANUARY.

All the whites, with the Governor in uniform at their head, attended at Cooper's funeral. It was very decently conducted, and really an affecting sight.

Hall, a ship carpenter, lately come out in the Company's service was buried the same day, and we are told, there was no small difficulty in getting hands sufficient to carry him to his Grave. Behold the difference of respect to a respectable Black Man (Cooper) and a worthless White (Hall).

A very hot morning. I was taken ill after my return from the Funeral and sent for and took an Emetic. I have been too much harassed in body and mind, for my present strength, for these last ten or twelve days - and this ravenous appetite which I got by my last illness has done me no good - adding to that the eating of Yams for breakfast and at afternoon coffee, which puffs me up, and makes me feel uncomfortable. Hang it Dawes! Why? Cannot we afford ourselves a bit of bread now and then man. The best way to keep a man's soul comfortable is having his body so - isn't it?

My mind is never easy while my body is a sufferer and it in my own power to relieve it - *proof of an affectionate* sympathely [sympathetic?] mind.

✑ FRIDAY 30TH JANUARY.

The Governor, Mr. Ludlam and Snr. Domingo went up to Granville Town today with the Boundary afresh. Having set myself to taking Bark for today, I did not accompany them - taking Bark lustily.

At Dinner the conversation turned upon having a newspaper. So a newspaper we must have.

Spoke with Smith about an exchange of 3 acres to square both our farms, in case it will suit Smith.

✑ SATURDAY 31ST JANUARY.

Taking Bark again today. I think this fever will stand a bad chance with such treatment. He [the fever?] making off with himself.

January (a reflection on the month). Dews have fallen by no means in such quantities this month as the last. The former part of the month was hazy and harmattanish; the Harmattans are doubtless, healthful, and bracing. This wind, which always blows from the East quarter, falls as the sun makes towards setting. And the air has a particular coldness sometimes even bordering upon keenness in the morning of a harmattan day. The Harmattan has been caught at 70°. The haze began to clear away during the last 3 or 4 days of the month. Pineapples are but just coming in. Pork is, at present, our most common dish - in the meat way. Fowls are very scarce; our beef which arrived at 'good order,' about a month ago has fallen away again most woefully,

[The last seven pages of this notebook are left blank]

[No entry from January 31, 1801 to May 31, 1801 inclusive, when June 1, 1801 begins a new notebook, the fourth. Is a notebook missing? There is no explanation in Book IV, stating why no entries have been made during this period, which is most atypical of Ross. We have seen, how, when he neglected his journal, through illness (from Thursday, December 11, through to the 22nd), he promptly explained to us what had happened.

A part of the explanation for Ross' silence is most certainly due to
the fact that during this period he was having great problems with the
government, and he, in fact, resigned his position as Superintendent
of the Maroons on May 27, 1801. His letter of resignation, addressed
to the Governor and Council, rather laconically said:]

Gentlemen,
You will be pleased to appoint to the office of
Superintendent of Maroons one in whom you may think
yourself safe to place more confidence than

Gentlemen
Your Most ob^t...Servt.
(Signed) George Ross.

[See also Appendix 1, Letter V]
*Now what led up to his resignation? From his journal it is clear that Ross
has been irritated over certain issues, the chief of which was his housing situation, where the authorities kept putting off the erection of a suitable abode
for him. The pettiness of certain officials and their general parsimoniousness
also irritated the superintendent. But Ross had a philosophical bent of mind
which made it easy for him to bear suffering with* sang froid. *And as he obviously displayed a persistent tendency not to expect too much from mankind,
this insulated him from extreme disappointments. But he probably felt that
he had reached the threshold of tolerance when he asked the government to supply him with 20 muskets and 10 lbs. of powder for the purpose 'of exercising
the Maroons,' and his request was flatly denied. The Governor and Council
resolved that they did 'not think it expedient to comply with the requisition
made by Mr. Ross for muskets for the use of the Maroons.' Ross' letter with
the request was written on May 26, 1801, and apparently the request was
denied the same day while his letter of resignation quoted above was dated
the following day. This by itself may not have triggered his resignation -
though there is no doubt that Ross took his position as superintendent of the
Maroons very seriously.*
*Concurrently with the above situation, Ross had received a letter from the
Secretary of the Governor and Council pertaining to Maroons' accounts
which Ross would seem to have interpreted as impugning his motives and
questioning his honesty. The letter rather clumsily said:*

Mr. Ross.

Sir,
Should you see nothing of remark in the accounts
communicated to you this morning which were sent in
consequence of the resolution of Council therewith
 transmitted you may return them.'

Signed A. Smith Secy.

*This letter was to be the cause of a very protracted communication between
Ross and Smith and Ross and the Governor and Council. (These letters are
to be found in Appendix I). Ross wrote to Smith, with spirit, to inquire about
the nature of the remarks the Governor and Council would have him make
on the accounts, at the same time writing also to the Governor and Council
wondering whether their secretary had spoken 'your mind on the subject - not
in the usual style of your language - I'm sure....' The reply to this came on the
same day as that refusing Ross the muskets. It said, rather tersely and with
a degree of asperity, 'that no person can with propriety call in question the
authenticity of a letter signed by the Secretary to the Governor and Council
in his official capacity.'*

*At this point Ross must have felt rather 'put upon.' Hence his resignation
which his* Journal, *as we know it, only mentioned indirectly in a lengthly letter; (entry of July 21, 1801 below). Ross also wrote a letter to the Board of
Directors of the Sierra Leone Company in London, explaining his resignation. (Appendix I, Letter VI)*

*His successor, Lieutenant Henry Odlum (mentioned casually in his June
1, 1801 entry only as Odlum) was first appointed,* pro tempore *at a salary
of £200 p.a. sterling by the Council but upon confirmation, his salary was
raised to £300,p.a.*

*As for Maroons' reaction to Ross' resignation and to his successor, we
know very little. The official documents are silent on this. Ross has left only
a passing reference to the possible reaction of the Maroons in his June 1,
1801 entry, when he wrote that the Governor tried to introduce Odlum to all
the Maroons at Granville Town, but the General told him that only '3 or 4'
turned up.*

✨ MONDAY 1ST JUNE.

Paying some Maroons today. I find the Governor has gone up to
Granville Town to introduce Odlum. He sent round to all the

Maroons but only 3 or 4 of them, the General says, attended.

Wrote to the Board for a Passage[64] and first opportunity and that till then I would live in my country hut.

⊘ *TUESDAY 2ND JUNE.*

In consequence of an appointment that followed a chat between Wilson and me on Saturday evening, I called on him after breakfast today. But nothing, I fear, is to be done. He says, I am welcome to his house, board, etc., in the meantime, and I may by and by, get some goods out.

I don't know! Something *I must do.* Received 2 resolutions from the Council. 1st, that I am to be allowed no passage home, there being no precedent, 2nd, that I am to be allowed £50 gratuity for my fatigue and exertions in settling the Maroons[65]

Saw Wilson again in the evening and had a fresh chat about a Brig that has just come down from Bance Island - as tho' I should go to Leeward in her - maybe so!

⊘ *WEDNESDAY 3RD JUNE.*

Dined at Gray's. Called on Wilson and saw this same Captain at his house - chatted with Wilson again in the evening.

⊘ *THURSDAY 4TH JUNE.*

I gave in my cash accounts today. A dinner at Government House and a ship in sight. I have got some fever again today. How is this?

⊘ *FRIDAY 5TH JUNE.*

This ship is the *Atalanta* and brings only letters from my father, Crispi, and Macaulay.

Dined at Wilson's, with Cummings and Hales and spoke to the latter after dinner upon the subject of my accompanying him down the Coast.

⊘ *SATURDAY 6TH JUNE.*

Received copies of minutes of Council in London respecting my salary and expenditures in America.[66] Oh, their meanness! Indeed, it is many degrees beyond meanness - it is injustice; it is downright robbery that they would practice on me -but it happens that I am but a poor subject - that's one comfort. So, out of their great care and kindness, and because I have done their business so well for them, they are graciously pleased to order that my salary of £140, shall, during my stay in America, be only £100 [p.a.?] So that after fagging away for them in cold and heat, in deaths and dangers, for near two years and conducting their business, not only with fidelity, but with great success, they will show me, when all is done, that my reward is the [?] being in debt! God! take up my cause. I did not deserve this at the hands of the Sierra Leone Company - thou knowest!

Wrote to the Governor and Council to have my accounts [67] settled as soon as possible and let me know the worst of it, as I meant going down the Coast in the *Hope*.

And Wilson too! Only last Tuesday you told me that if it were not for the scantiness of your supplies in trade articles, you would think it to my advantage to take up my abode with you. Yet tonight you shew me your stores, full of goods - so much so that you talk of supplying Car or Gray, tho' out of a most excellent Barter - but I hear not a word of 'my advantage in the change.' I don't think - but I'm too long in this world - in this Sierra Leone world, I certainly am. Hang it, 'tis a smoky house* and the sooner I'm out of it the better.

∾ SUNDAY 7TH JUNE.

To church in the morning. Smart came up the hill in the afternoon. Received a letter from Ludlam[68] in answer to mine of last night's wherein I expect he puts a more liberal construction on the explanation to the Directors respecting *necessary expenses* in America, than their same? [former?] explanation will bear.

∾ MONDAY 8TH JUNE.

Told Ludlam of a long string of my proceedings in Nova Scotia - reading Robertson's Scotland.

∾ TUESDAY 9TH JUNE.

Dined on board the *Atalanta*, Captain Cummings. Received minutes of Council in the evening stating that in consequence of my account of the business to Ludlam, and his to the Board, they referred its settlement to the Court of Directors, and there appeared £130 in my favour on my current account which I was at liberty to draw anytime.[69]

---

* see also pages 27 and 41.

⍦ WEDNESDAY 10TH JUNE.

I thanked the Governor and Council for the candid result of their consultations respecting the settlement of my accounts. Wrote to Dawes to let me have his account of what I owed him for the Mess, as I should get Wilson's.

Removed to Wilson's. Cummings from the Rio Pongas and Pickering dined there.

⍦ THURSDAY 11TH JUNE.

Sorting my things - always a dusty job and copied list of goods into Book.

⍦ FRIDAY 12TH JUNE.

Ludlam dined us and [?]; also Cummings and Hales.

⍦ SATURDAY 13TH JUNE.

Corankapone called on Wilson and I promised to note what I had heard him say - that the Mayor's Court ordered him merely as an officer of that Court, to go and fetch Zilpho[?] up?

Read Voltaire's play of Caesar by Franklin and compared to the incomparable Shakespeare, it is indeed a *poor thing*.

Hales dines with us and Wilson, after dinner, went on board -and got 2 men and a girl from him to be paid for in Iron at £8 a head - cheap indeed.[70]

So Gray talks of purchasing £2,000 worth of Hales goods, in which case, it seems likely that he will set aside his intended Leeward trip.

⍦ SUNDAY 14TH JUNE.

Having taken a pill last night, I kept the house today. Afternoon had some [?] of 31 years old at Hermitage's.

⍦ JUNE 15TH-22ND (INCLUSIVE).

At Wilson's, I have only to say that so much of my time is gone past. Received some letters from Bright on subject relative to the Maroons.

✑ *JUNE 22ND-29TH (INCLUSIVE)*.

Went to Bam (Bance) Island with Wilson and Hales the 25th, and back to Wilson's the 29th. Tilley was extremely polite to me while at Bam (Bance) Island, and Ballard is a fine fellow.

The *Anderson*, it is supposed (but not by me), will sail in the course of 6 weeks and Tilley takes his passage in her. She takes 150 tons of Camwood.

✑ *TUESDAY 30TH JUNE*.

I am sorry to learn that the Boat Tilley was so good as to send down with me yesterday, got upset last night on her way up - but fortunately no lives were lost, the poor fellows having stuck to the Boat's bottom, which was uppermost, all the way from near opposite Tagrin[?] to near opposite this place, where they were picked up. Is it not something that looks unkind in providence that Tilley should thus loose by obliging me? What can I say? this is certainly touching me in a tender part. I can bear what is commonly called hardships. I fancy myself armed at all points for hard and harsh treatment - but I am hurt - sadly hurt -when any person suffers by endeavouring to render me a service.

Cruel accident - were not my feelings, on account of Tilley's very great civilities - which I could not even indulge a hope of having an opportunity of making any return for, sufficient for me, without this addition? but I shall sit still and be quiet, and fortune may get tired of playing this game at [of?] football on my poor carcase.

✑ *JUNE (A REFLECTION ON THE MONTH)*.

Beginning of the month a good deal of rain, less about the middle but towards the latter end, nasty, gusty weather and not over healthful, I should suppose.

Winds mostly at from South to S.West.

✑ *JULY 1ST TO 8TH*.

I had a shocking afternoon of it yesterday with a pain about my stomach and bowels - 40 drops of Laudanum gave me a sleep.

Wilson returned today and indeed on several accounts I was glad to see him back. Oh dear! I was invited yesterday to dinner with His Excellency. Was it for this reason or on account of Odlum's illness that the Governor dined at Granville Town today?

✌ *FRIDAY 3RD JULY.*

Went out with Wilson in his boat to meet the *Lucy*, Captain Oldman. It was the *Lucy*, to be sure, but not Captain Oldman - poor Oldman had been killed by the slaves the 24th ulto; they having filed themselves out of iron, rose (and) killed the Captain and another and wounded the surgeon and others. Seven of the slaves were killed before the fray was settled.[71] There had been 73 on board - got at Goree - not 66. They sailed from Goree the 19th.

Smith[72], who has succeeded Oldman, says he left 100 more slaves on the island, which he could not purchase for want of Coral and amber. Chances like this should be the making of the Sierra Leone Company - their store should always have a sufficient assortment and Smith would now gladly, for the above articles, give them ivory, gum, wax and ostrich feathers.

Wilson too, loses by not having sufficient *store room* -50 tons of salt, Smith would let him have at about £75, which Wilson could pay for by less than 4 tons of rice - which he sells at £20 per ton. Now this 50 tons salt would at least bring Wilson 50 tons rice or maybe - a ton of ivory?

✌ *SATURDAY 4TH JULY.*

Took an excursion in Wilson's boat as far as the Cape and got wet this afternoon.

✌ *SUNDAY 5TH JULY.*

I was woke in the night by a pain in my stomach and in less than an hour I expected (it would) have sent me into the other world - Good God!

What extreme torture did my poor body endure for near one hour. I woke Jack and sent him to Leigh for some Laudanum and was relieved.

I slept till near 8 this morning and got hold of Buchan and made it out successively?[successfully?] that I had got an inflamation of the stomach - the pleurisy - peripneumony - and I don't know what all (sic) [unfinished sentence]

The fact, however, is that I let myself, about 3 weeks ago, go too long costive, and by leaving my windows open of a nasty wet night, got a cold on the back of that which cold I shamefully neglected - and yesterday I got wet and remained so till bed time and besides, when getting wet, ate half of a pineapple. I took 2 ozs. bitter purging salts and 10 drops Laudanum.

❧ MONDAY 6TH JULY.

Dr. Lind's remark on the climate of this Coast is just: That health is general for a considerable time at certain time and in the course of one week, perhaps of one night, several are laid up, probably carried off. Witness the soldiers and Maroons who have enjoyed such health, and of whom scarce one has died for several months until within the last week or fortnight, and now there are seven soldiers dead, besides 4 or 5 of their wives, and children; and of the Maroons, 3 have gone off since 3 o'clock this morning and many are very low and in danger.

Hales came down yesterday after having sold his slaves to Tilley and sent them up by the master of the Dowdeswill[?].

Four tons of Camwood he gets for his 17 slaves - with a prospect of a peau[?] which Tilley informs me there is. I think Master Hales has made a very indifferent market of his slaves -indeed, if there be a prospect of a peau[?] I should not think myself by any means safe(?) to give 50 pounds per ton for my camwood as Hales does - and of such an assortment as Hales has too, which certainly is a choice one.

Hales has got up today in Wilson's Eliza for his camwood and he says (he is going) to do more business with Tilley if he can.

❧ JULY 7TH TO 13TH.

In the course of this week Critihill of the *Hannah* came in without an anchor or cable on board, having lost 4 where he had been at Leeward - poor fellow, he has got only 35 tons of rice and half a ton of ivory.

It is boisterous weather to Leeward and the rice and pepper season is not for 4 or 6 weeks yet to come.

How much an owner loses by sending a master that does not know the trade! Poor Critihill thought he did well in getting six bars for his boxes of tobacco pipes. Box and pipes for 6 bars; and for rice too!

Leigh got knocked up this week too. The *Dowdeswill*, Captain Bronton [unintelligible] came down and sailed for Demarara (with) passengers M. Crandall and Nairn [?] from Bance Island - the latter having but 10 slaves after his years servitude [?] and going home now a figure more ghostly sure than Hamlet's representative.

On Sunday I assisted Hales in taking an account of his remains, and Sunday took a turn round the *Carpenter.*

The *Carpenter* I pronounce *one mile* distant from the Cape. The false Cape is in a direct line from the *Carpenter* to the highest land of the bananas - which line I take to be as nearly as possible due South and North. Seen next paper for Brinton Boat!

∾ *TUESDAY 14TH JULY.*

Session held today upon Thornton Hill. Aye, true about that Boat Wilson had of Brinton as it points out in a striking light the profits made by a trader sitting down in this part of the world.

He had the boat for £10; he offered for the £10 a Bill on London or Ivory in hand. The latter was accepted; the £10 or say, the boat, was paid for by 8 (elephants'?) teeth [unintelligible] if you please, weighing, in all, 48 lbs. - then he added a couple of goats as a dash. Now, upon recollection, Wilson found that the purchase of the Ivory in question cost him about 6 weeks ago, only £2. And he is sure that Carr will give him for the boat 2 teeth of 50 lbs.[?] each or that Johnston will give him 2 tons of camwood for it. So that at Carr's price his £2 will return him £25, and at Johnston's at the present rate of camwood, £100!

Oh shame, shame! Hales, how could you see that poor unfortunate man Doctor perish in his own nastiness - till the maggots were feasting on him while yet alive! I must allow that Wilson's indignation was just - for the neglect was cruelly inhuman.

Walked out with Wilson toward Carr's this afternoon.

∾ *WEDNESDAY 15TH JULY.*

Well said Judge Ludlam! Zilpa cannot be tried today -Zilpa - even she! Who is at present there in court, cannot be tried today - *because there is some informality in the drawing out of the Recognizance Bond* given for this appearance in court. Oh most righteous judge! A second Daniel too, no doubt.

[No entries for 16th and 17th July.]

∾ *SATURDAY 18TH JULY.*

I wrote to the Governor and Council today for bills for £100[73] Received [blotted] Governor Dawes' account of my mess on Thornton Hill leaving me 70 odd dollars in his debt.

✑ SUNDAY 19TH JULY.

Went out to look after the ship *Chance*[?] with Wilson and Hales in the *Eliza*, but she was not visible.

✑ MONDAY 20TH JULY.

Received a note from Bright saying I could not have money or bills until I had done so and so. Walked out toward Carr's in the afternoon.

Wrote a letter to Crispi to be left with Wilson for Critihill.

✑ TUESDAY 21ST JULY.

Hollo! here comes Carr with open mouth - what book is that he has got in his hand! His letter book - he has just been entering a copy of a letter sent by the Governor and Council on the *Duties*. There is a bill too, which the collector has sent him for Duties from the 23rd July last, amounting exclusively, of the *Susannah's* cargo.....

Gray grumbles too; that the colony is at present in the most defenseless state in which he has ever seen it, and in short, in every point of view, the most precarious in point of security.

Having a good deal of paper here which I am not likely to use, I may as well copy the letter I am about to send to the Governor and Council:

Gentlemen,

You have refused me a passage home - you refused to furnish me with a Statement of my Account and (notwithstanding there is a balance in my favor) you refuse to supply me with money - Such oppressive measures on your part I am well assured will not find their justification in any part of my conduct - You pretend too to adduce reasons for your proceedings - pray let us examine them. -

The lst is you require 'an exam.' of the Maroon accounts which have passed thro' my hands and a full report thereon'-

I answer to this that strictly speaking no Maroon accounts have passed thro' my hands except the acct. of Cash Kept by myself and which I delivered in to the accountant in due time but have not to this day heard anything more of it.

You know Govt. that neither the Maroon acct. nor the matters which constitute the subject of them were ever put under my direction - You therefore could not justly have demanded of me even while Superintendent of the Maroons, in the Company's service - You could not .- I say there have existed on what you now lay down as the grounds of proceedings the most unjustifiable.[?] But when the matter comes to be inquired into, it will be found that I was willing to wave (sic) the point of *right* and only requested to be informed respecting the nature of the remarks which you would have make on the accounts you sent me for inspection -

Govt,
I did not make such request without a cause - I shall state two - the manner in which the Maroon accounts were kept I had all along seen must in time lead to confusion, besides its leaving them open to error and imposition in the meantime, I was therefore in hopes that an answer (such an answer as might naturally be expected) to the request I made would lead to such an explanation or canvassing of the business as should afford me a fair opportunity of pointing out what was wrong in order to have it remedied in future.
The other cause which I promised to state is a very forcible one indeed; with me at least it was so. - The accounts in question are open to remarks which as a faithful servant of the Sierra Leone Coy. I conceive I should not be justified in making - The character however of an *honest man* was too dear to me to have passed them over in silence so long as my orders could be construed to bear that they ought to be taken notice of -
I must here beg leave to observe to you that what in your letter of yesterday you have called a 'full report' was only called so in your letter of yesterday - formerly it was wont to go by the term remarks - 'a full report' - Yes, I shall make a full report and a true report to the representatives of the S.L. Coy. here as well as in London - I meant no less - but I shall have the whole of the Maroon accounts before me to make this report and not a part of them - I shall not be told that there are some on 'which I need not report as my sentiments had been already collected verbally by Mr. Ludlam'.
The 2nd cause by which you would justify your conduct is that 'You first want a list of the names of the Maroons and Nova Scotian settlers among whom the Rebel premium money of Dr. 400 has been distributed with the sum paid to each person.'
Had I conceived there was any necessity for furnishing you with such a list, you should have had one at the time I gave in my accounts - or had I known you wanted one since that time, the aversion I naturally bear to Contention of every sort, and in every

shape would have induced me to furnish one - you will receive one enclosed -

The Maroons and Nova Scotians shared D^r.2.70 each; the boys a dollar a pair - There remained a fraction of 10 cents which in presence of all the Maroons was paid over to Jarrett in name of interest for a debt of one dollar owned him by the Maroons from Nova Scotia, of which debt I have had occasion to take notice elsewhere.

Your 3^d ostensive (sic) cause is (I am sorry you oblige me to say it) of a perfectly teasing and vexatious nature, and I have already given you all the satisfaction I was able to communicate on the subject by writing - Let me beg of you to consider the matter but for one moment, and you will not I am persuaded any more trouble me on (the) subject, without it is for the mere sake of giving trouble, which I should be glad to avoid thinking you capable of if possible -

You mention a distinct and special account of Mr. Ludlam's relative to this business - give me leave to hand to you, after having made a few remarks by way of elucidation.

I have now done Gentlemen - You may choose your future measures, but you shall be called to an account if God gives me life.

> Gentlemen,
> I am your most obedient
> George Ross
> July 21st, 1801

P.S. In the afternoon I received a few lines from M. Bright which certainly have every appearance of having been dictated in a confused dream on the subject - not as if the man was awake!

Having unsuccessfully asked for a passage home, Ross decided instead to go on a voyage with Tilley along the West African coast, possibly to trade, but for reasons not made clear, they were delayed for some time in Sierra Leone. He still kept a diary but now his entries are not regular. That of July 25th said, 'Here we are still hanging out - going every day but never any day gone - oh the dear pleasure of this sort of uncertainty!' Later in the entry, he showed his usual disappointment with the government of Sierra Leone: 'What shall I say more? What is there worth saying or noticing in this cut-throat place? I hear nothing all day but fresh instances of those miserable wretches of a Governor and Council making all about them as uncomfortable as they can.' And with a few more entries, with 16 blank pages remaining, notebook 4 came to an end. The last 3 of these pages, written with notebook turned upside down, had entries on certain dishonest practices on the part of the store keep-ers (June 24, 1801), which he headed 'Scraps on Store Proceedings,' but these are being omitted here.

The Gambia

Notebook 5, from Tuesday 4th August to 25th August 1801, has long, inter-esting entries on the Gambia and a few other West African ports. the Gambia is given the greatest attention (pp.1-38) which I shall paraphase although these pages are crossed through diagonally, with what appears to be a light blue crayon pencil - possibly done by an official of the Sierra Leone Company or by the Colonial Office, for reasons inexplicable.

Ross has some notes on the Gambia generally, reflecting on the nature of the soap he found there, which rises in salt water. He is obviously interested in their trade goods, promising to take a look at their cotton, indigo or blue dye; also the mahogany of which he is going to procure a sample. Then he begins his daily diary.

ᘒ *4TH AUGUST — 12TH AUGUST 1801.*
(A PARAPHRASE)

Here he has entered minute descriptions of the flora and fauna of the Gambia, also the shape of the houses - circular in form, very neat and thatched, with piazzas, and not too many windows; the houses are surrounded with fences, formed by a sort of bamboo to keep the wolves out, 'which are apt to come about the houses in the night and pick up their young ones.' On board, they had a visitor. Mamadoo Sambo, Chief of Soko, who 'rattled on board and cut not a few capers along with Captain Hales.' Mamadoo had his band of music along with him - the leader being only 6 feet 8 inches tall! But the chief soon 'got done over with ...liquor.' Ross noted the cultivation of rice and corn in the Gambia. On Wednesday, he was shooting pigeons and monkeys, admiring the many beautiful birds and apparently found the wasps and mosquitoes a nuisance, having complained of 10,000 bites from the latter. Saturday, August 8 found him dining with Mamadoo Sanse at his Palace, and 'an excellent dinner it was' - Goat mutton, which, 'I think I must be forced to own I never saw so fat - so sweet - so tender - so good' the rice, too, was excellent, and 'well pressed', and the Kus-kus was made of Indian corn. For pud-ding, they had a large calabash full of rice, dressed 'in a peculiar manner with lime juice and the fat of the mutton. Master mamadoo had too much good breeding to go to (sic) help me to some of this new dish with the same spoon that stood in the mutton calabash, without cleaning, tho' it was only taking it out of mutton grease to put it into mutton grease, so out he takes it, gives it three or four licks of his tongue and began helping me to the rice sans ceremonies.' for drinks, they had wine and port.

Ross, in observing the 'several large cornfields,' along the Gambian border, reflected that they were few in number in comparison to what they might have been: that is, if the number and ability of the natives, the goodness of the soil, the facility with which it may be cleared and cultivated, or the repeated experience of want and inconvenience which the people are plagued with about this time every year are all taken into consideration.

His august 12 entry had some interesting ethnographic descriptions of the Joloffs and the Mandingos. He visited a small Joloff and Mandingo settlement called Floop Town which, he said, was never yet visited by a white man, and apparently for this reason, Ross saw them as being in a very 'uncivilized state.' He said their language is called Floop and that they were Pagans 'in the most complete sense - they sell a good many slaves'. Their houses were perfect huts, they and their cattle lived together -which reminded him of the Highlands [Scottish?]; they have no writing - [this word is unintelligible but it could be gewel, the Wolof name for griot. If it is gewel, then it would not be accurate to say that the Wolofs did not have gewels - but Ross' next sentence complicates the issue further.] Commenting on the absence of writing, he compared this situation with himself -noting what a 'bitter thought' it would be were he to have had no writing or if writing could not come unaccompanied by [unintelligible]. then, said he, 'witness my poor Maroons.'

He said that the Floop people are to the N.W. of the Gambia and they, like the Mandingos, are Mohammedans but they are not very strict for they drink wine etc.

While long in bed from fatigue, there came Plena, a black girl - she came in softly and 'pressed her lovely lips incontinently to mine, by which I was abruptly waked out of a dream...-'Woke by a 'kiss'...and the 'black hussy...staring me broad in the face as she stood by my bedside...I startled as tho' I had been struck - in a moment I felt ashamed - she laughed - I could not help taking her with a spring full in my arms and giving the gypsie a hug.'

Ross was soon a lodger at Plena's house, which had been built two years previously by one Captain Anderson, who, 'poor fellow, died of fever.' Plena prepared 'fowls, cake and bread for supper.' Ross measured Plena's house which was 34 feet by 28 and the walls were '15 inches through.' 'And this house, I am told, was built two years ago for 2 slaves' money.'

Price Listings of Slaves

Ross' casual attitude to slavery is again demonstrated by his entry of August 12: 'Account of the Present Price of Slaves'. All these goods were trade items mediated by the iron bar, which was the medium of exchange for slaves.

2 Guns	Bars	12 Calculated at £1.4.0	
5 Bafts	50	" "	6.5.0
Amber	4	" "	0.12.0
Coral	4	" "	0.16.0
Gun Powder	13	" "	1.6.0
Tobacco	30	" "	0.10.0
Iron	4	" "	0.16.0
Breads	5	" "	0.5.0
Scarlet	2	" "	0.10.0
Flints	1	" "	0.1.0
Lead	1	" "	0.1.0
Snuff Boxes	2	" "	0.2.0
Pen Knives	2	" "	0.2.0

£12.10.0

+10/-for unforseens

£13.0.0

A note mentioned that Hales (a slave trader) sold his slaves for £8 a head at Sierra Leone - but 'they were not prime to be sure, but they were good and most of them prime.'

August 13 saw Ross at the cobbler's which he spelt 'Gobler'. Here 'the Gobler sewing one of my shoes and I did the other, and you shall hear me assert with the greatest seriousness - for serious truth it is, that my shoe was the best (sic) gobled of the two.' [August 25th 1801 saw the end of Ross' Journal. He is about to take a trip to

Vintain...'It is just in time for I have finished this Book and I have not another on this side Vintain.' If he continued his Journal while on the Coast and when he returned to England, there is no known record of this.[76]

The last seven pages (book turned upside down again) are taken up with a miscellaneous assortment - probably of every possible item of trade, meticulously and neatly drawn up with straight and horizontal lines, displaying a trained regard for the rules of the ledger system.]

APPENDICES

APPENDIX I

LETTER 1 [Ross' appointment to the Sierra Leone Company.]
The Governor and Council
Received a letter from Mr. George Ross in the Company's Service.

Freetown, 13th April 1797

Sir

Please to lay before the Governor and Council the following Memorial. viz.

That at a Council of Directors held at the Sierra Leone House London the 10th December 1795, I had had the honor to be informed by the chairman that 'I was from that day to consider myself a Servant of the Company.' In consequence thereof, and from the Concurrence of various Accounts having cause to suppose that it has been the Uniform practice of the Company to commence the Salaries of their Servants from the date of their Engagements; I humbly conceive my Salary ought to have commenced from the 10th day of Decem^r, and not from the 6th of January thereafter, as entered in the Books of the Accountant. I am your very Humb^l Servt

(Signed)
'George Ross'

[The Governor and Council resolved that there was a mistake with regard to Mr. Ross' salary and that he should be allowed salary from '10th December 1795, instead of the 6th January 1796.']

LETTER II (Ross' appointment as Superintendent of the Maroons, November 3, 1800.)

The Governor and Council

The important office of Superintendent of the Maroons being still vacant, though Mr. Ross has acted *ad interim* in that capacity, the Governor and Council met this day to fill it up. It was a subject which had frequently occupied their serious attention and they now without hesitation fixed upon Mr. George Ross as being best qualified to hold it from his personal knowledge of the Maroons, and having a claim of merit to the appointment by the influence he had obtained over them, and the satisfaction he had given to the Board by his communications upon every matter of inquiry concerning them. And as the Governor and Council were convinced of the propriety and expediency of rendering his situation among the Maroons both advantageous and respectable, they determined to put him at all times on a footing with the Senior Counsellor of the presidency in point of Salary; and to secure to him a due share of authority, they thought it advisable to invest him with the powers of Justice of the Peace, and the right of presiding in all judicial causes arising among the Maroons.

It was therefore resolved

I. That Mr. George Ross be appointed,and he is hereby appointed Superintendent of the Maroons with a Salary of £200 Sterling p.a.

II. That in point of Salary he be put at all times on a footing with the Senior Counsellor of the Presidency.

III. That Mr. Bright be requested to draw up a letter conveying the news of his appointment, and the powers that are vested thereof, together with a copy of these Resolutions. The Letter was as follows:

To George Ross Esquire, Superintendent of the Maroons

Thornton Hill, November 3, 1800

Sir,

I have the pleasure to inform you that the Governor and Council by a Resolution of this date, which I enclose have thought proper to nominate and appoint you Superintendent of the Maroons. By this appointment they convey to you a general superintending and controlling power over all persons belonging to the Colony. They invest you with the powers of a Justice of the Peace. You will have the appointment of Constables; and conforming in all cases, as far as circumstances render it advisable, to the spirit of the English law, and its mode of Trial, you will preside as Judge on all judicial occasions of importance. The regulations and orders whether general or special which proceed from the Board, as well as all acts of grace and favour which flow from hence will be communicated to the parties concerned through you; and particular attention will be paid to your recommendations. You will perceive Sir, by the few specifications here made that the Governor and Council are not disposed to be niggard of their confidence, and are sensible of the propriety of rendering your situation with the Maroons respectable and your authority over them efficient. For this purpose they are also aware of the necessity of assigning you a competent support, and they think themselves authorized to place you in this respect on a footing with the Senior Counsellor of this Presidency. His Salary is at present £200 (sterling)p.a.; it will probably be raised in the new Civil List to £300; yours it is proposed shall keep pace with his. You will have the additional advantage of living rent free. Whatever extraordinary expense necessarily attach to your situation under the article of Table expenses will be reimbursed to you; but of these, experience and your own discretion, must determine the amount. On your part the Board expect at all times a free and open disclosure of sentiment; and a return of that confidential communication which they shall be ever ready to impart; than which nothing can be more conducive to the public Good, or the personal satisfaction of both parties. More particular instructions must be referred to a season of more leisure and deliberation.

> By order of the Governor and Council
> (Signed) R^d. Bright,Sec^d in Council

Letter III [Ross' Letter complaining of his desperate Housing situation.]

The Governor and Council
Received a Letter from Mr. George Ross in the Company's service.

Thornton Hill, December 31, 1800

Gentlemen

As you were well acquainted with the circumstances, I could not have supposed that any application on my part would have been requisite to have my situation meliorated: far less than near 3 months should have elasped and repeated personal applications proved entirely fruitless. To the hardships which were thus imposed upon me, as well as the exertions which unavoidably fell to my share after the landing of the Maroons; and while I had no other assistance than what I could derive from themselves must certainly be attributed my present indisposition of now 5 weeks standing.

Having considered of the above matters with all the coolness I am capable of I now beg leave to state my resolution, that if it should please God Almighty to restore my health, no consideration will prevail with me again to take up my residence at Granville Town without my situation there is made such as to afford a reasonable hope of enjoying such a degree of health, as will enable me to perform the duties of my office. Should you determine upon my return to Granville Town, I will thank you to point out some place of residence for me in the meantime. I am etc.

(Signed)'George Ross'

The Governor and Council took the above into consideration, and resolved,

1. That however sensible the Governor and Council may be of the uncomfortableness of Mr. Ross' situation at Granville Town from the want of a decent house to reside in, and however much they have to lament his being so long and severely indisposed, which certainly may in a great measure be attributed to the causes he states, they are not aware that anything has been wanting that could be done on their part either to get him a proper house built or to meliorate his situation in other respects as far as lay in their power.

II. That the Master Builder having had express directions to get up the Maroons' storehouse, and also a house for Mr. Ross, with all the expedition he might be capable of has had his people almost solely employed on those works ever since the Maroons arrived, and that it is to be ascribed to the want of proper workmen that Mr. Ross' house is not up by this time.

III. That until Mr. Ross' house be completed, it be not required of him to reside amongst the Maroons at Granville Town, but that he do merely visit them occasionally as his business there may require or his health may permit.

IV. That from the inadequateness of the Company's buildings to accommodate their servants there is not a separate house in Freetown that could be assigned to Mr. Ross at present but in the meantime he be allowed the use of the apartment he now occupies in the government house.

LETTER IV [Ross' Letter of Resignation, May 27, 1801.] See p. 62.

The Governor and Council
Received a Letter from Mr. George Ross in the Company's service.

LETTER V

Thornton Hill, May 27, 1801
Gentlemen
This is meant to obviate every possibility of a doubt in regard to your receiving my letter of yesterday's date: likewise to say that I shall be far from having any objection to being accompanied to Granville Town by any Gentleman you may think proper to appoint; for which place I mean to set out in the course of about an hour or two hours at furtherst.
I have the honor to be

Gent^m Your most Ob^t Servt
(Signed) George Ross 9 o'clock.

LETTER VI [Ross' Letter to the Board of Directors, Sierra Leone Company, London, sent through the Governor and Council, on his Resignation, May 29, 1801.]

Gentlemen
You will oblige me by giving the enclosed a place in your first Dispatches to the Directors. I have sent it unsealed for your perusal.

> I am, Gentlemen,
> Your most Ob^t Humble Servt
> (Signed) George Ross.

Sierra Leone, 29th May 1801

Gentlemen
From the statement which you may receive of the circumstances which led to my giving up the superintendency of the Maroons, I think it is not improbable that my conduct may appear to you to have been hasty
I beg leave to say that it was in truth not a hasty but a deliberate and pre-determined sacrifice of the salary I had attached to that office, for the true interests of your colony. And it would afford me certainly the greatest satisfaction to be called upon to make it appear the same.
I was aware, Gentlemen, before I undertook the arduous station of Superintendent of Maroons (and indeed on the first outset it was a *most arduous one*). I say Gentlemen I was aware that I might not be entrusted with powers sufficient to do justice to the office; and repeatedly expressed myself so to Mr. Ludlam, who was Governor at the time. I however did undertake it with such powers as were thought proper to be vested in me for the time; but with the full and firm determination to resign it as soon as the time should arrive when for want of sufficient powers or any other wants on my part, I should apprehend the service to be likely to suffer - which determination I have also expressed to Mr. Ludlam and to others. That time, Gentlemen, lately arrived and I have acted up to my said determination.
To my earnest wish to be permitted to lay before you a particular and circumstantial account of the motives that led to every part of my conduct, I have only to add this remark, indeed a remark on the truth of which I could almost be satisfied to rest

the merits of my proceedings viz. that before 12 months go round matters will so fall out that it will appear the measures I would have adopted, had a sufficient degree of confidence been reposed in me, were *proper* and *necessary*. I allude particularly to *arms* and *accounts*. You may then - And may you then, Gentlemen (whatever becomes of me) reflect that you had a servant whose fault was not the being unfaithful to the interests of the Sierra Leone Company; nor his failing (I will say it) a want of discernment in regard to the most proper means to be adopted for the promotion of them, in so far as related to his own particular sphere of acting.

Wishing every success to the Sierra Leone Company most sincerely - And with grateful acknowledgements for the many favors I have had the honor of receiving at your hands. I beg leave to subscribe myself, Gentlemen, with the utmost respect.

Your most Ob^t and very H^b Serv^t(Signed) George Ross.

LETTER VII [Ross' letter to the Directors of the Sierra Leone Company, for a passage home to England.]

The Honorable the Chairman and Court of Directors, of the Sierra Leone Company, London (n.d.)

Gentlemen,

I beg leave to acquaint you that it is my intention to return to England by the earliest opportunity - And, I trust you will have the goodness on the part of the company to furnish me with a passage.

It may be well likewise to inform you that as soon as my affairs relative to the Maroons are settled (which I expect will be the case in a few days) I mean to remove to my own hut in the country; where if I shall be able to forward the service(?) during the remainder of my detention here I shall be very glad to do it.

I am Gentlemen,
Your most Ob^t Servant
(Signed) George Ross

LETTER VIII [Reply of the Governor and Council to Ross' letter asking for a passage home, June 2, 1801.]

I. Resolved that the Governor and Council do not think themselves authorized to allow to Mr. Ross the expenses of his passage to England, as they can find no precedent of such an allowance being made to persons resigning the service.

II. Resolved that a gratuity of £50 sterling be granted to Mr. Ross in consideration of the fatigue and exertions as well as the inconveniences in point of residence to which he was subject in settling the Maroons.

LETTER IX

[Letters and Minutes respecting Ross' salary and Expenditures while in Nova Scotia.]

Governor and Council

George Ross Esquire

Fort Thornton, 6th June 1801

Sir,

Herewith you will receive the copy of a resolution of the Governor and Council of the 5th instant: and also paragraph 43 of the Court's letter per Atalanta with the resolution of the Committee of trade referred to in the above paragraph.

Council, Fort Thornton, 5th June 1801

Resolved that by a resolution of November 3, 1800 it appears that Mr. George Ross is entitled to the same salary as the 1st in Council from the period at which any increase which the Court of Directors may think proper to make in the salaries of their servants, on the new civil establishment shall take place.

Court's Letter, March 24, 1801

Par: 43. By a resolution of the Committee of trade of the 10th instant, you will see what is our intention with respect to Mr. Ross' expenditure - from the time of his leaving England till he reached Sierra Leone. We wish you to ascertain what his necessary expenses during that time were; by which we mean his travelling expenses in this country; the expense of his passage to and from America; and his travelling expenses, and expense of board and lodging while in America. These you will allow him on account, superadding to them a salary at the rate of £100 a year for that time. To the period of his quitting England, his salary may be charged at £140, the rate at which he was engaged; he during that time being supposed to pay for his board and lodging.

APPENDIX II

[A series of letters dealing with accounts, some of which may appear trivial to us today. But not only do they throw much light on the personalities of early Sierra Leone history, but in a wider sense, they represent the parsimonious nature of British colonial practice in Africa, Asia and the West Indies.]

LETTER I
Letter from Alexander Smith to Ross, May 13, 1801.

'Mr. Ross' (sic)

Sir
Should you see nothing worthy of remark in the accounts communicated to you this morning which were sent in consequence of the resolution of Council therewith transmitted you may return them.

Signed A. Smith Secy.

LETTER II
(Ross' reply to above, May 13, 1801.)
The Governor and Council May 26, 1801

Letter from Mr. Ross, Superintendent of Maroons

                              Thornton Hill, May 13, 1801
Sir
Have the goodness to state the nature of the remarks the
Governor and Council would have me make on the accounts
you enclosed for my inspection.

                              I am Sir
                              Your very Humble Servant
                              Signed, George Ross,
                              Superintendent of Maroons

LETTER III [Ross' letter to Governor and Council questioning Smith's letter.]

The Governor and Council,

                              Thornton Hill, 13 May 1801
Gentlemen
I have this day received from your Secretary a Letter enclosing
some Maroon accounts from the store which he said were for my
inspection, and that if I should see anything worthy of remark
(I suppose he meant in those accounts) the Governor and
Council desired I would state it when I returned them.
Before I could satisfactorily as I conceived make such remarks
as might meet the intention of your requiring my inspection of
the said accounts I thought it necessary to request your
Secretary to have the goodness to state the nature of the
remarks, the Governor and Council would have made on those
accounts. The information I was honored with from your
Secretary Gentlemen, is an follows viz.
[That is, Letter I Appendix II, Smith to Ross, May 13, 1801.]

LETTER IV
(Reply of the Governor and Council to above.)

The Governor and Council

I. Resolved that it appears to be wholly unnecessary to point out the nature of the remarks which mr. Ross may see cause to make on the Maroon account.

II. Resolved that no person can with propriety call in question the authenticity of a letter signed by the Secretary to the Governor and Council in his official capacity.

III. Resolved that the Governor and Council do not think it expedient to comply with the requisition made by Mr. Ross for muskets for the use of the Maroons.

LETTER V
(Alexander Smith to Ross, (a Post Script) n.d.)

P.S. The Governor and Council desire to know when it will become convenient for you to lay before them any other Maroon accounts which you may have by you.

(Signed) A. Smith

LETTER VI (Ross' reply, June 5, 1801.)

Thornton Hill, 5th June 1801

Gentlemen

In consequence of a resolution of Council handed to me the 2nd instant whereby I learnt your determination not to furnish me with a passage to England, I have resolved upon going down the coast in the brig Hope, now lying in the harbour and which sails as I am informed on the 10th instant.

My reason for mentioning it is - that if possible I may not be prevented from proceeding by reason of my accounts not being settled.

Your Secretary mentions 'other Maroon accounts which I may have by me.' I should be glad to know what they are; for I certainly wish to have all my accounts with the Sierra Leone Company settled as soon as may be - Would to God it had been the case two twelve months ago! But I beg your pardon

Gentlemen, And I know you cannot but excuse me, when I inform you, that your secretary has just now handed me copies of resolutions of the honorable Directors respecting my salary and expenditures in Nova Scotia.

I have only to intreat, that I may know as soon as possible, the worst I have to expect for two years of most faithful and most arduous service in the extremes of climate.

> I am, Gentlemen, etc.
> (Signed) George Ross.

LETTER VII (The Governor and Council's reply to above.)
To Governor and Council
Reply read.

George Ross Esq.

Fort Thornton, 6th June 1801

Sir,

The lateness of the hour at which your letter ofthis date has been received prevents its being regularly taken into consideration by the Governor and Council; butas any delay in answering it would be improper, I shall reply to the most material parts of it with the concurrence of as many members of the board as are present.

With respect to the settlement of your private account, it is impossible to say anything determinate at present, as you have not yet furnished us with the means of settling it. The Court has ordered you to have credit for the amount of your necessary expenditure, in America and in England preparatory to going to America. And though they have used the words 'necessary expenditure'from the very liberal construction they have authorized us to put on that expression (by a paragraph in their letter to the Governor and Council a copy of which has been transmitted to you) no expense under the headsthey have specified can be deemed unnecessary which was consistent with the character you were bound to support as their representative in America. That these expenses should be specified is too reasonable to admit of a moment's doubt. If anything can add toits resonableness, it is, that there are expenses which probably will not be borne finally by the company and that proper vouchers will be therefore absolutely requisite. The Maroon accounts alluded to were some charges against the Maroon department sent in to the Governor and Council from the store; but which ought properly to have passed first thro' your hands, and were therefore transmitted to you; Mr. Fothergill's account and vouchers; Mr. Hermitage's if any have been sent to you, as I have been led to suppose might be the case; Mr. Leigh's as store-keeper to the time of your resignation, if they have been sent in, and such charges as you yourself may have to make on account of house rent and extraordinary expenses in consequence of the Governor and Council's letter to you of November 3rd 1800.

'T. Ludlam.'

Read this draft of a letter to Ross.

LETTER VIII

Fort Thornton, 9th June 1801

Mr. George Ross,

Sir,
The Governor and council on the verbal statement of Mr. Ludlam acquiesce in the reasons Mr. Ross has given for not rendering a written statement of the particulars of his expenses while resident in Nova Scotia. It is impossible for them however while not possessed of such a statement to act according to a resolution of the Court and they have therefore determined to refer the matter to the re-consideration of the directors, and this they do the more readily both because Mr. Ross will probably be soon in London and able personally to explain every circumstance relative to his situation in America: and because they are persuaded, that when the Court is fully acquainted with those circumstances which hitherto it cannot have known, it will be induced to revise the terms of its resolution with a favorable attention to Mr. Ross' services. The Governor and Council will not fail in their next letter to represent their sentiments on this subject to the Court: in the meantime they have ordered the sum of £290 at present at the debit of Mr. Ross' account, to be placed to account current London. It appears to have been the intention of the Court of Directors, that the salary of the

Superintendent of Maroons including all allowances, should be
£300 they have directed that a credit at that rate be given to Mr.
Ross accordingly.

By order etc.
(Signed) A. Smith.

P.S. It appears from a statement of your A/C (account) laid
before the Board by the Accountant that - the sum standing to
your credit, and which you will be at liberty to draw for is £130
stg. A.S.

Governor and Council approved of the contents of the said Letter
and Resolved that it be transmitted to Mr. Ross as the determination
of the board, and that the acting Accountant be instructed to conform
thereto.

Resolved that in conformity with the Resolution of Court of
Directors, respecting the Maroon establishment, the Superintendent
of Maroons salary 'be fixed at £300 stg. including all allowances for
table etc; to start June 1, 1801 with Lieu. H. Odlum

Resolved that the Superintendent of Maroons be authorized to provide Col. Montague James with a few necessary articles of household
furniture.' Mr. James Flangnam be appointed Storekeeper to the
Maroons at £30 V. Mr. William Leigh.

LETTER IX
(Ross's letter of thanks in reply to above, June 10, 1801.)

The Governor and Council, June 12, 1801
Received a letter from Ross in the Company's service.

Thornton Hill, 10th June 1801
Gentlemen
I beg leave to thank you for the very candid result of your delib-
erations respecting the settlement of my accounts with the
Company. To Mr. Ludlam my thanks are particularly due, who
had the goodness to hear my verbal account, and interested
himself so far as to represent his view of the subject to the board.
This being meant merely as a letter of thanks, it may perhaps
be rather out of character to add, that I have great confidence

that the more thoroughly my conduct is investigated, the fairer will be the light in which it shall appear.

I am etc,
(Signed) George Ross

(Council meeting, June 27, 1801. Richard Bright, now Second in Council, reported on the 'several letters' between him and Ross. They were read and inserted in the Minutes.)

LETTER X (Bright's letter to Ross, June 17, 1801 asking for evidence of his having given the Maroons and a few Nova Scotians the sum of $400.00 for their part in quelling the Rebellion.)

George Ross Esq.

Fort Thornton, June 17, 1801
Sir,
Among the accounts of expenditure for the Maroons transmitted by you to the Governor and Council no mention is made of the sum of 400 Dollars given (pursuant to a resolution of the 7th March) to be distributed by you to Maroons who bore arms against the rebels, nor of the reservation of equal shares for the 6 Nova Scotians who acted as guides to the Maroons, specified in the said resolution the substance of which was transmitted you in a letter of the 30th March last. The Governor and Council have ordered me to transmit for your examination the accounts of Mr. Leigh as Storekeeper; and those of the commercial agent; and they request you to examine and report thereon. They think it unnecessary to give you any further trouble respecting Mr. Fothergill's accounts, as you have already verbally remarked thereon to Mr. Ludlam.

By Order
Signed R^d Bright
Second in Council.

LETTER XI (Ross's reply to above.)

R^d Bright Esq.

June 16th 1801

Sir,

It is true that in my accounts of expenditure for the Maroons I have made no mention of D^s400 given to certain persons who bore arms against the rebels-neither have I made any mention of another sum (D^s 156.067 I think it was) allowed by the Governor and Council to certain Maroons for losses sustained on board of the Asia. My reason was that I did not think it necessary; nor indeed strictly proper. Both the above sums have been truly paid with an exception of 2.70 Dollars the premium of George Ogram (he never having called for it) and which I will thank you for the Governor and Council to receive from the Bearer.

I should be glad to be favoured with a statement of my account with the Company as soon as it may be convenient.

I am etc.
(Signed) George Ross.

LETTER XII [Bright is insisting on vouchers.]

Fort Thornton, June 17th 1801

Sir,

Unless Governor and Council have a voucher from you for the payment of D156.067 allowed to certain Maroons for losses by them sustained on board the Asia, they will not be able to make good their claim upon the British government. I beg leave to add that the documents you have sent in contain no information respecting the lands that may have been procured by you for the Maroons as subsidiary to their town lots. Every particular respecting them it will be necessary to state explicitly; as the quantity of land, the term for which it is held, of whom procured, the actual tenants, and the rent to be paid.

By Order,
(Signed) R^d Bright
Second in Council.

LETTER XIII [Bright is further insisting on vouchers in a second letter.]

George Ross Esq.

Fort Thornton, June 18, 1801

Sir,

I am sorry to trouble you further on the subject of accounts, but I cannot omit transcribing part of paragraph from the Court's letter per Atalanta, to shew the necessity of a voucher to every account out of which a claim may arise on the British Government.

Such accounts as it will be necessary to present to Government ought to be accompanied by vouchers, and formally attested by the proper officer and also by our Governor.

(Signed) R^d Bright
Second in Council.

LETTER XIV [Bright is asking for public papers in Ross's Possession.]

George Ross Esq.

Fort Thornton, June 19, 1801

Sir,

The Governor and Council request that you will cause to be delivered at the Secretary's office, all papers of a public nature now in your possession respecting the Maroons, and especially the plans of the town and country lots.

By order
R^d Bright,
Second in Council.

LETTER XV [Ross's reply and public papers sent.]

Rd. Bright Esq.

Freetown, June 19th 1801

Sir,
The Bearer is sent with the public papers I had in possession
respecting the Maroons.
The Governor and Council must know that the Surveyor is the
proper person to apply to for any plans they may want of the
country allotments.
A plan showing the number of the town lots I have sent as I am
aware it could not be furnished by any other and the want of it
would be attended with inconvenience.
I have as yet received no statement of my account with the
Company.

> I am etc.
> (Signed)
> George Ross.

LETTER XVI [The letters are becoming more heated.]

George Ross Esquire

Fort Thornton, June 20, 1801
Sir,
By order of the Governor and Council I remit you your statement of the losses sustained by individual Maroons in wearing
apparel etc. on board the Asia, that you may write in ink the sum
total which at present is only in pencil; and also indorse on the
said statement: 'The sum total contained in this statement was
truly paid by me' - Signed by you as Superintendent.
I am likewise ordered to say that the statement of your account
with the Company will be delivered to you whenever you chuse
to attest the examination of the several maroon accounts that
have passed through your hands, or make your report upon any
errors contained in them; the governor and council regarding
this as your indispensible duty.
They also require of you a voucher for the payment of the distribution money to the Maroons for the apprehension of rebel

settlers; likewise a specification of the subsidiary lands which you have procured for the Maroons.

By order,
(Signed) Richard Bright
Second in Council.

LETTER XVII [Ross's reply to above.]

Ross to Bright

Freetown, June 22, 1801

Sir,

You multiply letters but do not appear to have at all made yourself acquainted with the subject on which you write. Had you taken the trouble to look into the Vouchers delivered in by me some 3 or 4 weeks since, you must have found among them Receipts regualarly drawn out and signed by the several persons who received money for losses sustained on board the Asia.

I have also to observe to you, that the statement you have sent being an imperfect one ought not to be remitted for any such purpose as that you intimate. You might have remembered that I delivered in another and a more compleat statement of a latter date than that you have sent - indeed you should have known that any statement not amounting to the total sum specified by the receipts ought not to be considered as compleat.

You 'are ordered to say that a statement of my account with the Company will be delivered to me when I chuse to attest the - examination of the several Maroon accounts that have passed through my hands or make my report upon any errors contained in them, the Governor and Council regarding this as my indispensible duty.' I answer that with regard to my account with the Company the Governor and Council may do as they think proper. They are not likely to be troubled with anymore applications from me on the subject, for from their determination in such cases I am aware that *here* there is no appeal - but, Sir, on the question of 'my duty' give me leave to say that *I shall take the decision with all its consequence* upon myself and I will be plain to tell the Governor and Council that the line of conduct I have chalked out for myself in regard to the Maroon accounts, is, to reserve my sentiments on the subject while in Sierra Leone; fully believing that however much it might be for the Company's or for Government's interest that they should have been stated and acted upon while I remained at the head of the

Maroon department; and when I wished for an opportunity of doing it; yet, that by doing it now or before I shall have left the Colony I must do injustice to the subject and probably to myself.

I have already said that the rebel premium-money had been truly paid-if any further voucher is necessary you must be at the trouble of specifying it.

I have likewise declared the subsidiary land 'procured by me for the Maroons to be three acres of Thomas Jackson at a dollar per acre for a year.'

I remain etc.

(Signed) 'George Ross

LETTER XVIII [Bright to Ross, asking for premium money receipts.]

George Ross Esquire

Fort Thornton, June 22, 1801

Sir,

The Governor and Council desired you to send per Bearer the accounts handed you for revision on Saturday last. For the opportunity given you of stating your sentiments in regard to the Maroon accounts they must refer you to their resolution of the 8th of May and their Secretary's letter of the 13th of the same month.

The Receipts you mention are among the Vouchers; they had been overlooked.

Receipts of the same kind should have been taken for the distribution of the Rebel premium money.

By order
(Signed) Richard Bright
Second in Council

LETTER XIX [Ross is asking for bills.]

The Governor and Council

Freetown, July 18, 1801.

Gentlemen

I will thank you to furnish me with bills on the Directors for £100 in one of £50 and 2 of £25 each.

I am etc.
(Signed) George Ross

LETTER XX [Numerous demands for bills etc. before above can be met.]

George Ross Esq.

Fort Thornton, July 20, 1801

Sir,

In answer to your letter of the 18th inst: I have it in command from the Governor and Council to say, that they cannot grant you the bills you require on the Court of Directors; or pay you the balance of your account until you comply with the following demands, viz.

I. An examination of the Maroon accounts which have passed through your hands and a full report thereon.

II. A List of the names of those Maroons and Nova Scotian Settlers among whom the rebel premium money of four hundred Dollars has been distributed with the sum paid to each person.

III. A distinct and particular statement of each parcel of land assigned by you to Individuals or families among the Maroons as subsidiary to their town-lots, specifying the lot to which each parcel belonged. The numbers of these lots with the names of their actual or probable proprietors were delivered to you distinctly and specifically by Mr. Ludlam.

Till you comply with these requisitions, the Governor and Council will not think themselves justified in answering your demands for any larger sum than may be necessary to defray the expense of your passage to England.

By order
(Signed) R^d Bright 2^d in Coun^l

LETTER XXI [Ross's uncharacteristically long letter of July 21, 1801, justifying his conduct with respect to Maroon accounts.]

The Governor and Council

Freetown, July 21, 1801

Gentlemen

I. You have refused me a passage home - You refused to furnish me with a statement of my account - and notwithstanding there is a balance in my favour you refuse to supply me with money - Such oppressive measures on your part I am well assured will never find their justification in any part of my conduct. You pretend too to adduce reasons for your proceedings - pray let us examine them.

II. The 1st is you require an examination of the Maroon accounts which have passed through my hands and a full report thereon.

III. I answer to this, that strictly speaking *no Maroon accounts* have *passed through my hands* except the *account* of *cash* kept *by myself* and which I delivered in to the Accountant in due time, but have not to this day heard anything more of it.

IV. You know, Gentlemen, that neither the Maroon accounts nor the matter which constitutes the subject of them were ever put under my direction. You could not therefore justly have demanded of me - even while Superintendent of Maroons, in the Company's service - You could not I say then have insisted on what you now lay down as the ground of proceedings the most unjustifiable.

V. But when the matter comes to be inquired into it will be found that I was willing to wave (sic) the point or right and only requested to be informed respecting the nature of the remarks which you would have me make on the accounts you sent me for inspection and to make my remarks on.

VI. Gentlemen, I did not make such request without a cause - I shall state two.

VII. 1st the manner in which the Maroon Accounts were kept I had all along seen must in time lead to confusion, besides that it left them open to errors and imposition in the meantime. I therefore was in hopes that an answer *(such an answer as might naturally be expected)* to the request I made, would lead to such an explanation or canvassing of the business as would afford me a fair opportunity of pointing out what was wrong in order to have it remedied in future.

VIII. The other cause which I promised to state is a very forcible one indeed - with me at least it was so - The accounts in question are open to remarks which as a faithful servant of the Sierra Leone Company I conceive, I should not be justified in making. The character however of an honest man was too dear to me to have passed them over in silence so long as my orders could be construed to bear, that they should be taken notice of.

IX. I must here beg leave to remind you that what in your letter of yesterday you have called a full report was only called so in your letter of yesterday; formerly it was wont to go by the term 'Remarks' - 'A full report' - yes, I shall make a full report, and a true report, at the desire of the Representatives of the Sierre Leone Company, here as well as in England - I meant no less - but I shall have the whole of the Maroon accounts before me to make this report on, and not part of them. I shall not be told that there are some 'on which I need not report as my sentiments had been collected verbally by Mr. Ludlam.'

X. The 2^d cause you adduce for your refusal of Money is that you first want 'a list of the names of the Maroons & Nova Scotian Settlers among whom the rebel premium money of D^s400 has been distributed with the sum paid to each person.'

XI. Had I conceived that it was all necessary to furnish you with such a list you should have had one at the time I gave in my accounts - or had I known you wanted it since that time, the aversion I naturally bear to contention of every sort, and in every shape would have induced me to furnish one. You will find one inclosed.

XII. The Maroons & Nova Scotians shared D^s2.70 each, the boys had a dollar apiece and there were ten cents over, which in presence of all the Maroons were paid over to Jarrett under the name of 'interest for a debt of one dollar owing him by the Maroons from Nova Scotia'; this debt I have had occasion to take notice of elsewhere.

XIII. Your 3rd ostensive (sic) cause (I am sorry you oblige me to observe it) is of a perfectly teasing & vexatious nature, and I have already given you all the satisfaction I was able to communicate by writing on the subject - let me beg of you to consider the matter for a matter & what I have said on it, and you will assuredly not trouble me anymore on the subject without it is for the mere sake of giving trouble, which I should be glad to avoid thinking you capable of, if possible.

XIV. You mention a distinct & specificial account of Mr. Ludlam's relative to this business - give me leave to hand it you herewith, after making a few remarks on it, by way of elucidation - I have now done, Gentlemen, you may chuse your future measures, but you shall be called to an account if God gives me life.

I am etc
(Signed) George Ross

'Appendix' (sic) to above Letter

Remarks on a letter from Mr. George Ross to the Governor and Council dated the 21st of July, 1801.

Par. 1.The Grant of a passage home to a person who has resigned the service, the Governor and Council regard as a matter, not of right; but of favour or special agreement. It is a favour surely, which no servant of the Company is warranted to expect, who without previous notice of his intention or any regard to the detriment it may occasion to the Company's interests, vacates a situation of high trust and great political importance.

The Grounds for withholding the statement of Mr. Ross's account are given in the Board's letter of the 20th of June, wherein Mr. Ross is expressly told that the Governor and Council regard the examination of the several Maroon accounts that have passed through his hands as his indispensible duty. To this Mr. Ross replies 'that on the question of duty he shall take the decision with its consequences upon himself.' The most material consequence that can follow this decision is the refusal to pay him the balance of his account. It should be observed that the greater part, or perhaps the whole of this balance has arisen from the desire of the Governor and Council to view Mr. Ross's former services and exertions in the most favourable point of view. The gratuity of £50, the increase of his salary to £300 per annum; and their resolution respecting his expenses in America were matters of favour, not of right; and were indeed favours granted at a time when his late conduct had given them great and just cause of dissatisfaction; which nevertheless they would not suffer to efface the impression his former services had made. He himself admits their adjustment of his account to have been liberal: And the immediate return he makes for this liberality is to refuse to perform a material part of his duty; a part of it, it may be remarked which he was required to perform for the general good of the service, and the credit of the Company: not the ease, or convenience, or advantage of the Governor and Council. The Governor and Council do not hesitate to declare their opinion, that Mr. Ross has consequently forfeited not only his claim to extraordinary favours; but to the remainder of the ordinary remuneration for his services (should any be due) so long as he persists in with holding so important a part of those services.

Pars. 3&4. The Accounts in question were put into the hands of Mr. Ross (whether by the persons who drew them out, or by the Governor and Council is surely immaterial) to undergo all the examination which his opportunities of information enabled him to give.

Par. 5: Mr. Ross's request to be informed respecting the nature of the remarks he was desired to make was captious and futile: he had been told to state *any thing* worthy of remark in the Maroon accounts.

Pars:7.8.& 9. The cause stated in the 7th and 8th paragraphs are of great moment. The Governor and Council think Mr. Ross inexcusable for not stating them at first; and chargeable with gross neglect of duty in refusing to act upon them since; when so many opportunities have offered and requisitions been made to that effect. The distinction between a faithful servant of the Company and an honest man reflects no credit on Mr. Ross. The Governor and Council protest against the adoption of such distinctions on any occasion; and especially when pleaded in excuse of wilful and repeated contempt of duty.

Does Mr. Ross in the passage alluded to mean to imply that the Conduct of the Company or of their principal and accredited Servants will not bear light? and that an honest man with liberty to remark on the Maroon accounts would in point of conscience be compelled to take such notice of them, 'as a faithful servant of the Company,' not having the like permission would deem inconsistent with his duty: If it were so, the cause of the objection did not exist: Mr. Ross had liberty to remark; to make any remarks; and has been since urged and required at three distinct intervals of time both to remark and *report* on the Maroon accounts. Having dropt the character of 'a faithful servant of the Company' does Mr. Ross reserve that of 'an honest man' to play it off with more eclat against his late employers at home? This intention Mr. Ross seems to avow in the conclusion of his ninth paragraph.

Par. 11: It is usual with Mr. Ross to assign a very compendious though a very unsatisfactory cause for disobeying an order, viz. that he conceives the matter injoined not to be *necessary* nor *strictly speaking proper.*

Par. 13: The thirteenth paragraph of Mr. Ross's letter throws no light upon a question involving property in land to an unknown account, and valuable from its proximity to Granville Town. The distribution of this land was intrusted solely to Mr. Ross who will not even so much as name the individuals or families among whom it was parcelled out. What a train is here laid for jarring claims and interminable disputes. To conclude, the Governor and Council have given upon every proper occasion unequivocal proofs of their disposition to conduct themselves towards Mr. Ross not only with justice but with liberality. Witness their mode of conferring on him the office of Superintendent, the salary originally & subsequently annexed to it: the due regard paid to Mr. Ross's sentiments on various points of service; the gratuity voted him in compensation for the hardships and inconveniences he underwent in settling the Maroons; and lastly their measures for carrying into effect and perhaps going beyond the liberal intentions of the Court of Directors in settling his account. The conduct of Mr. Ross indeed, since that period, has forfeited all claim to favour, but the stipulated price of this services is only withheld on account of the non-performance of his duty.

Alexander Smith.

LETTER XXII [Bright to Ross for Fothergill's accounts.]

George Ross Esq.

Fort Thornton, July 21, 1801

Sir

If you have not a copy of Mr. Fothergill's accounts (which is a matter not clarly stated in your letter of this date) they shall be forthwith handed to you, as well as such other accounts as you may want in order to report thereon.

In case they should be needed, you are requested to return them as soon as you conveniently can.

By Order
(Signed) R^d Bright 2^d in Coun^l

[It is not clear how these seemingly petty account questions were finally resolved. We also have not been able to trace Ross's activities after we last saw him travelling along the West Coast of Africa and dabbling in the slave trade. After his return to Britain he probably lapsed into anonymity.]

FOOTNOTES

1. Shyllon, Black People, pp. 152–153.

2. Captain Smith, one of the many Smiths to be encountered in this journal, was one of the Maroon officials. He Fought bravely in the 1795 Maroon War in Jamaica and was given the option to remain in Jamaica but decided to leave with his colleagues to Nova Scotia.

3. Another Maroon character, who was apparently rather old by the time he embarked for Sierra Leone. He died just under a month after reaching the colony, leaving heirs behind.

4. General Montague James, the leader of the maroons, is referred to most of the times as 'the General' by Ross. For a biographical sketch of him, see the Introduction, and notes.

5. Lieutenant John Sheriff of H. M. Navy Commanded the *Asia* and was in charge of provisions.

6. This steward was old John Jarrett, a Maroon. But Winks would seem to make him out as 'a Nova Scotian Negro of Loyalist descent.' See Winks, *Blacks In Canada*, p.94.

7. Another Maroon.

8. See note 5.

9. Lieutenant Smith was the son of the British novelist, Charlotte Smith, which made Henry Thornton wonder if Smith had found any 'beauteous African at Sierra Leone. I suppose his mother will publish a new Novel.' His stint in Sierra Leone may not have given his mother matter for a new novel, but his part in the insurrection upon landing in Freetown certainly gained him distinction and honor. The Governor and Council praised him for his military skill and sent a letter to the directors of the Sierra Leone Company in London hoping that they would promote Smith. He was promoted and later knighted, and as Sir Lionel Smith, he eventually served as Governor, first of Barbados and then of Jamaica, being very successful in the former post but a failure in the latter for complicated reasons. For his career in Jamaica, See Mavis C. Campbell, *The Bynamics of Change in a Slave Society: A Sociopolitical History of Jamaica, 1800-1865*, Teaneck and London: Fairleigh Dickinson University Press, 1976, pp. 178-190.

10. Another Maroon.

11. Many hundred grand thanks.

12. Jarrett proved so disagreeable that the Maroons refused to let him be among the officers to wait upon the Governor when they arrived at Sierra Leone.

13. Another of the Smiths to be encountered. Corporal Smith was an English soldier.

14. Flogging was a common means of punishment among the Maroons, and this reference was probably to a father chastizing a son.

15. Elsy Jarrett was a part of the extended family of old Major Jarrett. It is not clear whether she was a daughter or a niece. The family must have been rather well-off judged by the amount of personal belongings they brought with them. See Campbell, *Nova Scotia and the Fighting Maroons...*p.164.

16. Shaw is already mentioned in the Introduction, as a part of the family that donated the land for the Maroon Church in Freetown.

17. The rather obscure tale to follow would seem to suggest that old Jarrett was indeed the father of Elsy who was beaten up (given the thumping) by Barnet while she was apparently *enciente* for Shaw. Barnet's thumping of Elsy was apparently due to unrequited love and all this took place in Preston, Nova Scotia, but because the child was prematurely born, Jarrett's vow is intimating that Barnet's beating may have had something to do with it.

18. Theophilus Chamberlain was first appointed Surveyor of the Maroons in Nova Scotia, and later became their superintendent.

19. The Cape Verde Islands off the Coast of Senegal, North of Sierra Leone; a Portuguese possession.

20. Palmer must have had some prescience of what was to come for his beloved dog died almost a month later. See entry of Wednesday, October 15.

21. A small island slightly north east of the Cape Verde Islands.

22. Another small island.

23. And yet another of these small islands off the coast of West Africa. St. Jago also goes by the name of Santiago - all a part of the Cape Verde Archipelago.

24. It was the practice of the period, upon citing and naming a ship, to enter the Captain's name.

25. This should be Fogo - an island in the Cape Verde group: Christopher Fyfe to author, April 9, 1978.

26. The Bananas are islands off the Sierra Leone Coast, center of the Slave Trade during that period. Originally owned by the Clevelands - a family of mixed African and English ancestry, but rivalries soon developed over the Bananas, between the Clevelands and the Caulkers.

27. Thomas Cox, an employee of the Sierra Leone Company, was Assistant Commercial Agent at a salary of £150. p.a., but became Mayor when the company received its Charter in November 1800, constituting Sierra Leone a Colony. Cox was shot dead a year later, defending Freetown from a Temne attack.

28. See Headnotes.

29. John Gray was Commercial Agent for the Sierra Leone Company at a salary of £300. p.a. when Zachary Macaulay was Governor. But before long, Gray, along with other employees of the S.L. Company, gave up their appointments and became Slave Traders on the West Coast of Africa.

30. Thomas Fothergill, whose name Ross would insist on rendering 'Fothingill,' clerk of the S.L. Company, was appointed storekeeper for the Maroons at a salary of £100. p.a., in November, but resigned February 1801, pleading his situation to have been 'extremely inconvenient.' He was succeeded by William Leigh.

31. Thomas Ludlam was Second in Council under Macaulay's Governorship, at a salary of £211 p.a. Ross's exclamation, 'no...don't' after his name, and subsequent references to him certainly showed that Ross did not have too high an opinion of Ludlam who had succeeded Macaulay as Governor when Ross arrived with the Maroons. Ross probably had good reasons for derogating Ludlam, described by one source as possessing neither theory nor practice for the position. See Thorpe, *A letter to William Wilberforce...*, p.12, while Fyfe saw him as 'a young man of twenty three without experience of governing or of Africa.' Christopher Fyfe, *A History of Sierra Leone*, p.76. And of the Africans, Ludlam thought that abolition of itself would not prevent them 'from still remaining a savage and uncivilized people.' Thrope, p.18.

32. This is Alexander Macaulay (brother of Zachary) who was first a ship's captain in the Sierra Leone Company service. He resigned and took command of the *Asia*.

33. Michael MacMillan was a schoolmaster in the employ of the Sierra Leone Company at a Salary of £50.00 p.a.

34. Richard Bright, fresh from England, was appointed a member of the Council under Ludlam's governorship. As second in Council in 1801, he and Ross conducted a long series of communication, found in Appendix 11.

35.& 36. Pickering and Viner may have been under-clerks or private soldiers.

37. The Maroons were said to have welcomed the occasion to be engaged in battle.

38. The terms were the rules, proposed by the Company, by which the Maroons were to be governed while in Sierra Leone. The Maroons refused to sign the document, but were understood to have acceded to it verbally.

39. Zimiri or Zimrie Armstrong was one of the Nova Scotians in favor of the rebellion against the Sierra Leone Government.

40. Ross's unfinished sentence was bashfully referring to the weeds among the coffee plants.

41. Granville Town, named after Granville Sharpe, was the original name of the Settlement of Freetown. Later, a part of what is now Cline Town was renamed Granville Town, after the first one was burnt down by King Jimmy.

42. It must be noted that African resistance to slavery began on the West Coast of Africa. Some ran away from different European factories or castles; others, the result of successful mutinies, returned to the coast, establishing runaway communities - or Maroon societies in the vernacular of the New World.

43. This was a copy of the charter from London, which instituted Sierra Leone a colony. The original copy was officially received by Governor Ludlam on November 6, 1800, which Ross has recorded.

44. It should be noted that at the time Ross was writing his journal the slave trade was in full swing, although increasingly under attack from the abolitionists in England.

45. This letter has not been traced in the official documents, but the lettrer appointing him Superintendent of the Maroons is full of praise for him. See Appendix I, Letter II.

46. Apparently Pickering has been promoted to the post of accountant.

47. Without doubt, Ross is correct.

48. In mid-Atlantic the *Asia* had captured the *El Angel* a Spanish ship, and all on board including the Maroons, received prizes.

49. Ross was in the habit of drilling the Maroons but later when he asked the government for more muskets for doing so, he was refused, and this was to contribute to his eventual resignation.

50. The answer was soon given to Ross when the Governor and Council authorized him to pay back the Maroons either in kind, as far as practicable, and if desired, or in money. For a comprehensive listing of the baggage the Maroons brought from Nova Scotia, see Campbell, *Nove Scotia and the Fighting Maroons*, pp. 163-249.

51. King Tom, one of the rulers of the Temme people, was the local ruler from whom the British bought the area of land to be named the Province of Freedom, now Freetown.

52. Ross's ethnocentric disgust would seem to be at its strongest when the Maroons would insist on burying their dead in their own way - with the beating of drums, for example.

53. As siad earlier, most of the Maroons - at least the leaders -were of the Akan speaking group originally from Ghana, and Colonel Montague was obviously of this group. But the term Koromantyn, variously rendered Koromantee, Koromantine, among others, has often been used indistinguishably from the Akan people, because of the Fante town, Koromantyn, from which many Africans were shipped to the New World.

54. Another of the Smiths. Alexander Smith was soon to be made Secretary to the Governor and Council.

55. The old Maroons were polygamous and certainly would not wish to change their ways but the government passed laws repeatedly for the 'effectual prevention of polygamy' among them.

56. It is not clear whether this is the same Bird who was apothecary to the Maroons, upon Dr. Chadwick's resignation.

57. Numerous references have been made by historians of iniquitous behavious in high places during the early history of Freetown.

58. Richard Corankapone (sometimes Crankapone, Crankepone) and John Kizell (mentioned above) were two Nova Scotians.

59. Ross painted a rather favourable picture of the Maroons in this report.

60. Boetifeur or Botifeur was a slave trader on the coast possibly of French extract.

61. Anderson, one of the leaders of the rebellion, was hanged as was Francis Patrick, another Nova Scotian, for their part in the uprising.

62. William Dawes, first sent out to Sierra Leone as assistant to Clarkson, soon became Governor, 1793-96, and had just returned for another stint.

63. The Maroons' attitude to the paying of quit-rent is discussed in the Introduction.

64. See Appendix I. Letter VII.

65. *Ibid.*, Letter VIII.

66. *Ibid.*, Letter IX.

67. See Appendix II, Letter VI.

68. *Ibid.*, Letter VII.

69. *Ibid.*, Letter VIII.

70. Ross became increasingly interested in trade and like most of the employees of the Sierra Leone Company, this meant the slave trade for which he showed no moral concern whatsoever.

71. This is one of the few successful Mutinies of a slave ship, but sad to say, the survivors were re-enslaved.

72. This may have been Alexander Smith, Governor's secretary, who was succeeded by Richard Bright, Second in Council.

73. See Appendix II, Letter VIII.

74. The official documents have this letter on record but with slight variations, here and there: See Appendix II, Letter XX.

75. Floop is one of the many names used by Europeans in describing the Fula or Fulani people.

76. Robin Winks has made reference to 'the first of five volumes' of the 'Diaries of George Ross,' in *Blacks in Canada*, p. 94 n 73. But in communicating with him and with Christopher Fyfe, and in consulting the documents, we are assured of only one diary.

Index

Article for Provision 16
the American ii, v-vi, xxii, 13
Anderson, Captain 76
the Anderson 17, 67, 111
The Arethusa 10-11
Armstrong, Zimiri 109
the Arthuran Frigate 10
the Asia 1, 6, 19, 21-22, 30, 33, 43-44, 47-48, 53, 87, 94, 96-97, 108, 110
the Asprey 21, 29, 31, 35, 46, 53
the Atalanta 64-65, 86, 95

Baily, Nanny 48
Baily, Venus 46
Bananas 11, 70, 108
Bance Island 64, 67, 69
bark 36, 46, 53-54, 61
Barnet, Hugh 58
Barnet, William 28
Barnet, Yago 49-50
Barrett, Goodwin 44
Boetifeur 50, 111
Bonard, Daniel 43
Brava 12-13
Bright, Richard 93, 97-98, 109, 111
Bronton, Captain 69
Brown, Bob *xiii,* 29
Brown, Tom 59
Bucknor, Cuffee 53
Bucknor, David 41, 58
Bucknor, Tom 41
Bullom *xi,* 15, 26

Campbell, Mavis C. *xxi-xxii, xxiv,* 106
Cape Verde 9, 107-108
the Carpenter 11, 69-70
Chadwick, Dr. 24, 28, 110
Chamberlain, Theophilus 107
Chambers, Polly 49
the Chance vi, 71
charter *v,* 21, 29, 31, 33-34, 49, 59, 108-109
Corankapone 47, 66, 110
Council *v, vii-viii, xvi, xx, xxiv,* 16, 21, 29, 31-36, 41, 47, 50-54, 57, 62-66, 70-71, 73, 79-84, 86-100, 102-104, 106, 108-111
Cox, Thomas 21, 108
Crandall, M. 69
Crispi 29, 53, 64, 71
Cummings, Captain 65

Demarara 69
Domingo, Snr. 61
the Dowdeswill 69

the Eliza 71
Ellis, Ann 50
Ellis, John 27, 37, 44, 50

Floop Town 75
Forbes, Alex 58
Freetown *i, v, x-xii, xiv, xvii-xviii, xxiv,* 19, 22, 32, 35, 39, 41, 49-51, 79, 83, 96-97, 99-100, 106-110

Gale, William 58
Gambia 74-75
Goree 10, 68
Gray, John 108
Gray, Peggy 47

Halifax 1, 4, 8, 16, 25
Hamilton, Nash *xvii*, 23, 57
Harding, Boyse 35
Harding, D. 24
Harding, John 48
Harding, Tom 30
Harris, Captain 21
Hawkyand, Secretary 6
Heath, D. 51, 58
Heath, Richard 58
Hermitage 20, 23, 25, 28-29, 31,
    33-35, 38-40, 42, 44, 46, 48,
    50, 52, 54, 66, 91
the Hope 65, 89
Horton, Sam 58, 60

Jamaica *i, iii, xv, xviii, xxii, xxiv,*
    18, 24, 106
James, Montague or the
    General, xiv–xvii, xxiv
James, Sam 38
Jarrett, Elsy 7, 107
Jarrett, Hobart 38
Jarrett, Miss 30
the John of Liberpool 50
Johnson, Colonel 30, 37-38, 43
Johnston 24, 58, 70
Johnston, Becky 58
Joloffs 75

Kizell, John 110

Laurice, James 30
Linton, Kitty 51
the Liberpool 50
lots 17, 33-34, 37-40, 43, 56-60,

    94-96, 99
the Lucy 68
Macaulay, Zachary *xxiv*, 108
MacMillan, Michael 108
Mandingos 75
Mayo 9-10
McNair, Captain 53
the Mercury 45
Morgan, Thomas 58
Morrison, Archy 53
Murphy, Mamadoo 35

the Nancy 55-56
Nova Scotia *i, v, x, xiii-xiv, xvi-*
    xix, xxii, 1, 23, 32, 65, 73, 86,
    90-91, 101, 106-107, 110

Odlum, Lieutenant Henry 63
Oldman, Captain 68

Palmer, Captain 2, 22, 51, 53
Palmer, Tom 30
Parkinson, John 58
Parkinson, Thomas 58
Plantain Islands 48
Praya Bay 10
Preston, Nova Scotia 107

Quit rent *xiv*, 57-58

Reid, Tom 39, 46, 55
Richard, Tom 44

Sambo, Mamadoo 35, 74
Sanse, Mamadoo 74
Schuman, Joseph 4
Sellars, Captain John 45
Sewell, Nelly 21
Sewell, Sam 24
Shaw, Charles *xviii*, 7, 16, 29, 37
Shaw, D. 23, 27, 37
Shaw, Sam xiii, 29, 37-38, 58

Singer, Robert 49
Slaves *ii, vi, viii, xv, xviii,* 68-69, 75-76
Smith, Alexander (Governor's Smith) 21, 33, 87, 89, 104, 110-111
Smith, Captain (a Maroon) 1-4, 6, 12-13, 16, 20, 23-24, 27-28, 31, 38, 41, 44, 51, 59, 106
Smith, Corporal 6, 107
Smith, Coup 46
Smith, Lieutenant, 1-4, 12, 23, 33, 106
St. Helena 10
St. Jago 9-10, 12-13, 107
St. Nicholas 9
St. Thomas 18
Stone, Hutchins 43
Stone, Phibe 29
Stone, Sam 9, 30
the Stranger 41, 52
the Susannah 71

Thompson, John, 49
Thompson's Bay 17

Thornton Hill 17, 19, 23, 37, 53, 70, 80, 82-83, 88-89, 92
Thorpe, John *xvii-xviii*
Thorpe, Sam 26, 57
Tilley 67, 69, 73
Tolley 17, 24
Tom, King *xi,* 27-28, 30, 40, 110
Tom, Prince 39

Vintain 76-77

Watts, Captain 35, 46, 48
Wheeton 59
Williams, Cyrus 24
Williams, Fanny 27-28
Williams, Herbert 57
Williams, J. 58
Wilson, James 21
Wolofs 75
Woolly, Captain 10
Wright, Robert 58